ALSO BY FRANCIS SPUFFORD

I May Be Some Time:
Ice and the English Imagination

The Child That Books Built

A Life in Reading

METROPOLITAN BOOKS

Henry Holt and Company, New York

THE

CHILD

THAT

BOOKS

BUILT

. . .

FRANCIS SPUFFORD

Metropolitan Books
Henry Holt and Company, LLC
Publishers since 1866
115 West 18th Street
New York, New York 10011

Metropolitan Books™ is a registered
trademark of Henry Holt and Company, LLC.

Originally published in the United Kingdom in 2002
by Faber and Faber, London.

Library of Congress Cataloging-in-Publication data
Spufford, Francis, 1964–
    The child that books built : a life in reading / Francis Spufford—1st ed.
        p. cm.
    Originally published: London : Faber and Faber, 2002.
    ISBN 0-8050-7215-2
    1. Spufford, Francis, 1964—Books and reading. 2. Children—Books and
reading—English—History—20th century. 3. Teenagers—Books and reading—
England—History—20th century. 4. Books and reading—Psychological aspects.
5. Children's literature—Psychological aspects. 6. Young adult literature—
Psychological aspects. 7. Fiction—Psychological aspects. I. Title.
Z1037.A1 S74 2002
028.5'5'0942—dc21   2002067834

Henry Holt books are available for special promotions and
premiums. For details contact: Director, Special Markets.

First Edition 2002
Designed by Fritz Metsch
Printed in the United States of America
1 3 5 7 9 10 8 6 4 2

CONTENTS

. . .

THE CHILD THAT
BOOKS BUILT

CHAPTER ONE

Confessions of an English Fiction Eater

■   ■   ■

"I can always tell when you're reading somewhere in the house," my mother used to say. "There's a special silence, a *reading* silence." I never heard it, this extra degree of hush that somehow traveled through walls and ceilings to announce that my seven-year-old self had become about as absent as a present person could be. The silence went both ways. As my concentration on the story in my hands took hold, all sounds faded away. My ears closed. I didn't imagine the process of the cutoff like a shutter dropping, or as a narrowing of the pink canals leading inside, each waxy cartilaginous passage irising tight like some deft alien doorway in *Star Trek*. It seemed more hydraulic than that. Deep in the mysterious ductwork an adjustment had taken place with the least possible actual movement, an adjustment chiefly of pressure. There was an airlock in there. It sealed to the outside so that it could open to the inside. The silence that fell on the noises of people and traffic and dogs allowed an inner door to open to the book's data, its script of sound. There was a brief stage of transition in between, when I'd hear the text's soundtrack poking through the fabric of the house's real murmur, like the moment of passage on the edge of sleep where your legs jerk as your mind switches over from instructing solid limbs to governing the phantom body that runs and dances in dreams. Then, flat on my front with my chin on my hands or curled in a chair like a prawn, I'd be gone. I didn't hear doorbells ring, I didn't hear suppertime called, I didn't notice footsteps approaching of the adult who'd come to retrieve me. They had to shout "Francis!" near my head or, laughing, "Chocolate!"

I laughed too. Reading catatonically wasn't something I chose to do, it just happened, and if it could be my funny characteristic in the family, a trademark oddity my parents were affectionate toward, that was great. Though I never framed the thought on the surface of my mind, stopping my ears with fiction was non-negotiable. There were things to block out. My parents were loquacious like me, constant reassurers, constant interrupters. Swags of talk flowed out of them like those many-folded banners used in medieval pictures, ancestors of the speech bubble. I idolized them and I wanted them to shut up. My little sister had kidney failure and trailed plastic tubes; I loved my ill sister and felt that I owed such a lot of attention to her state that I had better pay none. So treating the way I read jokily got us all off the hook. With an unspoken *whew* of relief it domesticated what was obviously a bit too extreme for comfort.

I still do it, still automatically wrap in humor my sludgy dives into text. I realized recently that in bookshops I do a placatory dumbshow as I move among the shelves. I've got a little repertoire designed to make my reactions to the books I'm cruising among *likable,* likable to an imaginary audience. Here I go, then: I'm in the basement of a big science-fiction bookshop in central London, jinking left and right past posters of Princess Leia, *Dr. Who* videos, Bart Simpson T-shirts, leather-fetish magazines mixed up in a rack with the *Fortean Times,* past science fiction's outworks of nonverbal and semiverbal stuff, toward its actual fiction, A–Z by author. My business is there, and when it comes to books I'm a really skilled browser, believe me, finely attuned to the obscure signals sent out by the spines of paperbacks, able to detect at speed the four or five titles in a bay that pull at me in different ways. What's this? Imported American military SF, black gloss cover with display type of gothic spikiness, picture of space-opera interstellar dreadnought encrusted with guns on the front. Keyword "mercenary" in the blurb on the back, so it'll be nasty; phrasing of the come-on lines also suggests post–Robert Heinlein right-wing libertarian blow-up-Oklahoma-City mad gun-toting bullshit, not an uncommon ideological flavoring in this subgenre, so it'll be programmatically nasty. I don't want to read this book, I certainly don't want to buy it, but I do want to take a single sip of its particular poison. Open a page at random. Oh my Lord, gushing human intestines. Very disgusting—yet also kind of arresting. But now I want to put the book back, and as I slide it back into its neon nest I also want to push it away from me, from my tastes and the kind of person I am. I want to demonstrate that between a person like me and a book like that only an amused disdain is possible. So I do this *thing*. I pantomime furrowing my brow in pain; I draw back my lips from my teeth like an affronted chimp; I push air against my upper palate to make a hissy, glottal-stopped disgust-noise. "Eekh!" I say, as if eyes were fixed on me from all quarters—as if the alacrity I now want to cancel might have been seen, like a spark arcing between eye and page, by other browsers, or the punks serving behind the counters who are often scholars of comic-book history, or the polite Asian heavies doing security at the door.

Actually, of course, I take it for granted that it hasn't. One of the first things you learn as you begin to read is the amazing exterior invisibility of all the rush of event and image that narrative pours through you. I'm thirty-two years old as I do my little performance in the bookshop, which means I've been reading for twenty-six years. Twenty-six years since the furze of black marks between the covers of *The Hobbit* grew lucid, and released a dragon. Twenty-six years therefore since the primary discovery that the dragon remained internal to me. Inside my head, Smaug hurtled, lava gold, scaly green. And nothing showed. Wars, jokes, torrents of faces would fill me from other books, as I read on, and none of that would show either. It made a kind of intangible shoplifting possible, I realized when I was eleven or so. If your memory was OK you could descend on a bookshop—a big enough one so that the staff wouldn't hassle a browser—and steal the contents of books by reading them. I drank down *1984* while loitering in the O section of the giant Heffers store in Cambridge. When I was full I carried the slopping vessel of my attention carefully out of the shop. Nobody at the cash desks could tell that I now contained Winston Smith's telescreen chanting its victories, O'Brien's voice admitting that the Thought Police got him a long time ago. It took me three successive Saturdays to steal the whole novel. But I have not ceased to be amazed at the invisibility I depend on. Other people can't see what so permeates me, I accept that, but why can't they? It fills me. The imbalance between what's felt and what shows means I carry the sensory load of fiction like a secret. Perhaps like all secrets it leaks in the end, but while I'm still freshly distended with my cargo of images, while I'm a fish tank with a new shoal in me, with one aspect of myself I enjoy the power of being different behind my unbetraying face. If I hung about stoned in front of a police station, solemn on the outside and spiraling chemically within, or wore a lace thong to the office beneath my business suit, I wouldn't be getting a different buzz. I flirt with discovery. My rigmarole in the SF bookshop is exhibitionism as well as defense, asks to be noticed while it tries to camouflage. Look at me! (Don't look at me!) I'm cramming myself over here, I'm gobbling worlds!

I need fiction. I'm an addict. This is not a figure of speech. I don't quite read a novel a day, but I certainly read some of a novel every day, and usually some of several. There is always a heap of opened paperbacks facedown near the bed, always something current on the kitchen table to reach for over coffee when I wake up. Colonies of prose have formed in the bathroom and in the dimness of the upstairs landing, so that I don't go without text even in the leftover spaces of the house where I spend least time. When I'm tired and therefore indecisive, last thing at night, it can take half an hour to choose the book I am going to have with me while I brush my teeth. It always matters which book I pick up. I can be happy with an essay or a history if it interlaces like a narrative, if its author uses fact or impression to make a storylike sense, but fiction is king, fiction is the true stuff, compared to which nonfiction is a shadow, sometimes appealing for its shadiness and halfway status; only the endless multiplicity of fiction is a problem, in a life where reading time is still limited no matter how many commitments of work or friendship I am willing to ditch in favor of the pages.

It isn't that I have the ambition to read *everything*. (Imagine the cultural moments when people could, though. Imagine that it's 1950 in the newly formed state of Israel, and you're up to date with every single touchingly unpracticed novel written in modern Hebrew, every radiant line of every poem that has used the typographers' new stocks of aleph, bet, and mem so far. Imagine feeling your mind sleekly stocked with all the reading there *is,* like a cupboard of perfectly folded linen. You'd be ready for anything.) No, the difficulty is that when you're conscious of the mass of fictional possibilities extending away and away, to choose between becomes a lengthier and lengthier task. How to settle on a particular straw in the haystack? A gradual, melancholy paralysis sets in. The more you see a bookshop how I tend to, as a chemist's dispensing an almost universal range of mood-altering substances, each slightly different from the next, the more essentially interchangeable books seem. The promise of reading recedes.

But I don't let go of it even when its satisfactions seem to be dissolving. I don't give it up. It is entwined too deeply with my history, it has been forming the way I see for too long. And I have a cultural sanction for my addiction. Books get cited over and over as the virtuous term of a contrast whose wicked other half is Nintendo, or MTV, or the Web. The villain varies but it's always some cathode-ray entertainment that jitters on the retina, where printed words are supposed to rest calmly. It doesn't matter that my eyes track across the breakfast table for the wafer of text on the cornflake box just as avidly as any channel hopper squeezing the remote, both of us eager for the mere brush of our chosen medium going by. The difference of the forms is enough. (They do work differently, of course.) In a world washed to and fro by glassy floods of representations, I choose to gaze at experience through the mesh of paragraphs. "The sky above the port was the color of television, tuned to a dead channel": first sentence of William Gibson's *Neuromancer.* If I see it instead as the color of wood pulp with printing on it, if what I see interposed between my eye and that evening gray is a history of the *verbal* descriptions of the sky, from Wordsworth's cloudscapes to Eliot's patient etherized upon a table—well, that makes me rather classy. The medium *I'm* wrapped in scores me a cultural point. I don't watch daytime soap operas, I'm bookish: I have the dignity of high culture, although in fact I find the frictionless surfaces of genre fiction easier food for my compulsion, and have to urge myself on through a George Eliot novel—no matter how much I'm enjoying it—by calculating the pages that're still to go. I have dignity, although in public places, after the phase of placatory self-consciousness is past, I sink into oblivion as I read, and come to rest in random postures. Once in a public library my attention was caught while I bent down to the lowest shelf of biographies. Time passed—a quarter of an hour, half an hour? My head was tilted way over on one side, and all the saliva in my mouth flowed into the cheek on the down side. Then someone visible only as a pair of legs coughed Excuse me. Sorry, I said thickly. As I moved back to the vertical to get out of her route to the lives of Sherman, Shostakovich, and Schubert, the spittoon overflowed, and I dribbled extensively on the carpet tile at her feet.

Most people would think I was missing something important in treating books as the kind of object you consume. *The wise man points to the moon,* runs the Chinese proverb, *but the fool looks at the finger.* Perhaps in seeing the people and events represented in the stories I read as so much flavored material, I am gazing at the finger instead of turning in the direction offered to me. And perhaps such a willful refusal of stories' representational depths and spaces makes it inevitable that their content should seem to fade on me. A great part of the power of fiction rests on its ability to indicate, to point out truths once we allow it to work as an arena for people like ourselves, who happen to be imaginary. Jane Austen does not deliver a sensation, like pistachio in the mouth or water on the skin, in describing Miss Bates in *Emma*. The finite number of paragraphs, observations, and spoken exchanges devoted to Miss Bates convey the compound experience of being familiar with her, with a person who is exasperating and vulnerable. The reader may feel the sensations of pity or irritation or fondness, but those are reactions. The business of the book is the creation of the figure we react to. It points her out. Look: Miss Bates, over there.

Our reverence for books, too, has really not much to do with them requiring deeper concentration than *Mortal Kombat*. It is the directions they can point us in that we value—and then the way those interact deep down in our reading minds with the directions our own temperaments are tentatively taking. Once books were sacred, literally: the regime of reading was set by the experience of reading scripture. But in the secular times of the last three centuries, which brought us printed words on every subject, print to screw into a ball and flip away after a single reading sometimes, the promise of revelation has splintered, and the splinters have fallen separately, without losing all of their original brightness. One smithereen (at least) has glimmered in the novel. With its conventions that mimic the three dimensions of the world off the page, and its simulation of time passing as measured by experience's ordinary clocks, we hope it can bring a fully uttered clarity to the living we do, which is, we know, so hard to disentangle and articulate. And when it does, when a fiction does trip a profound recognition—of the eddy current running counter to the main flow of a marital argument, which can lead one of you suddenly to cry out your admiration for the quality in the other that you've just been berating—the reward is more than an inert item of knowledge. The book becomes part of the history of our self-understanding. The stories that mean most to us join the process by which we come to be securely our own. Literacy allows access to a huge force for development. When an adult in a remote village rejoices that ABC is mastered, it isn't just because books bring the world to them; books bring them, in new ways, to themselves.

If the new reader is a child the situation seems even more charged with promise. We grow yet more certain that the book in the hand is a tool of growth. Fiction's onward movement fuses there, not with the ordinary traffic of our existence, but with the accelerated coming-to-be we do in childhood. Story's lucidating way with experience rushes into the primary fashioning of a self, the very first construction of a person out of the materials of environment, and family, and reading silence. This degree of inwardness is what truly leads us to value the book for children so high, at least in theory; over the video game, over the entertainments that can flood the forebrain, but deliver to the place under the skin where identity is kept only color and sound. The association between books for children and autonomy for children is very strong. When I told someone I meant to write about the dangers of childhood reading, "Good grief yes," she snapped with instant sarcasm, "before you know it they'll be thinking for themselves." And memory confirms it, for many of those who were eager readers as children remain eager-reading adults. We can remember readings that acted like transformations. There were times when a particular book, like a seed crystal, dropped into our minds when they were exactly ready for it, like a supersaturated solution, and suddenly we changed. Suddenly a thousand crystals of perception of our own formed, the original insight of the story ordering whole arrays of discoveries inside us, into winking accuracy.

None of this sounds like the footing for an addiction. Can you *be* addicted to discovery? If you were, would it be a problem? I know that, as someone who spent childhood falling into a book at every possible opportunity, I'm far from alone: there are a lot of us about, and for most of us it was an experience to rejoice in, not to worry about. The dominant sensation of reading was excited delight, as books did for us on the scale of our childhoods what the propagandists of the Enlightenment promised that all books could do for everyone, everywhere. They freed us from the limitations of having just one life with one point of view; they let us see beyond the horizon of our own circumstances. William Hazlitt said, "Books alone teach us to judge of truth and good in the abstract: without a knowledge of things at a distance from us, we judge like savages or animals from our senses and appetites alone; but by the aid of books and of an intercourse with the world of ideas, we are purified, raised, ennobled from savages into intellectual and rational beings." Adjust for the fact that the book in question will be Blyton's *The Island of Adventure* instead of Hume's *A Treatise of Human Nature,* and Hazlitt's manifesto applies. The books you read as a child brought you sights you hadn't seen yourself, scents you hadn't smelled, sounds you hadn't heard. They introduced you to people you hadn't met, and helped you to sample ways of being that would never have occurred to you. And the result was, if not an "intellectual and rational being," then somebody who was enriched by the knowledge that their own particular life only occupied one little space in a much bigger world of possibilities.

This is how I remember reading being too, nine-tenths of the time. But I want to know why I read as a child with such a frantic appetite, why I sucked the words off the page with such an edge of desperation. In a way, of course, I'm looking in the wrong place if I expect the books I've read to tell me that. No addiction is ever explained by examining the drug. The drug didn't cause the need. A tour of a brewery won't explain why somebody became an alcoholic. It wasn't any property of electric bells that made Pavlov's dog drool.

Nor does it necessarily prove anything about *books* that my reading childhood was succeeded by a tuned-out adulthood. In fact every account of addiction that lets the thing the addict craves provide the plot, in a sense tells the wrong story; or at any rate tells a half-story, made up of effects without causes. Thomas De Quincey's *Confessions of an English Opium Eater* does not tell you why De Quincey turned to laudanum, except by the inferential means of putting you amid the circumstances of his addiction. You can see that taking opium fills a hungry gap in De Quincey's life; you can learn the dimensions of the gap from the fact that opium fits it. But you can't learn why the gap is there. Beneath the chemical bliss he was willing to describe, beneath the nightmares where burning faces fused like the birds and fishes in an Escher drawing, lay levels of privacy he would not unlock. Which is natural: confessions always have limits, and it's easier to reveal spectacular indignities than to grope among origins. Perhaps the causes of De Quincey's addiction lay at a level that was not accessible to him either, pooled with all the chaotic and primitive aspects of himself that refused to be marshaled by his protective eloquence. They certainly lay far away in his life from the chemistry of opium.

Likewise I know that I have to look elsewhere in my life than the nature of prose to find the origins of my reading habit.

I was three when my sister Bridget was born. She was a small baby. Instead of following the nice upward graph of weight gain and turning into a rosy, compact toddler, she puked and thinned out. Instead of hitting the developmental milestones, and sitting up, and crawling, she just lay there. Her bones started to show through. By the time she was a few months old it was clear that something was wrong, but it took the doctors quite a while to come up with a diagnosis, because the odds were so long against the particular biological booby prize she had won. My parents were not related by blood. They came from different parts of the country. They had nothing obvious in common physically, except height and shortsightedness, and a certain earnest bearing. My mother had disconcerted the male students who wanted to seduce her when she was twenty, by not knowing the rules of the game: not so much resisting, as failing to notice that there was something to resist. At the same age my father had been frequently mistaken for a curate, which will happen if you go into a pub in a steel town when you're on an industrial-archaeology field trip, and order yourself a half-pint of lemonade to drink. But it turned out that they shared something else. Lost and unnoticed somewhere on the million-base braid of their DNA, both carried an identical sequence of Gs, As, Ts, and Cs. The sequence was recessive—it produced no symptoms in the carrier, and it would remain inactive if they had a child with anyone who didn't also have it. Put together two carriers, on the other hand, and each time a sperm fertilized an egg you silently rolled a dice. I was lucky: I only inherited the trait in the same passive form that my parents had it. Bridget wasn't. In her the sequence activated, coding for an error in the body's ability to process an amino acid called cystine. Instead of waste cystine being flushed out of her tissues, it accumulated, as crystals. It accumulated fastest of all in the organs that were supposed to act as filters, her kidneys. There were only about twenty other living sufferers in Britain, only a few hundred in the world; and most of *them* were found in a cluster in the Appalachians, where hillbillies had been upping the odds by marrying their cousins for generation after generation. It was a ridiculously rare disease, a disaster it was almost absurd to be afflicted by, like being struck by a meteorite. By the time that the Great Ormond Street Children's Hospital in London made the connection between Bridget's failure to thrive, and the condition called "cystinosis" that appeared in the obscure footnotes of medical literature, she had one kidney already defunct, and the other about to give in. It was the autumn of 1967. Only a little time before, she'd have died right then. But the hospital had an experimental therapy that might offer her a few years of life. They offered a plan that would keep her on, but not over, the brink of starvation. My parents threw themselves into doing what was necessary. They crawled out of bed hourly during the night to adjust the tube that fed sugar water, drop by individual drop, up Bridget's nose, down her throat past her gag reflex, and straight into her stomach. They coaxed her into taking a daily fistful of pills. They did the four-hour return rail journey to London again and again. My father held down his junior teaching job at the university. They ran a gigantic overdraft. They made it up as they went along. They were brave. Family photographs from the time show them gray-skinned with fatigue, but always smiling, always determinedly broadcasting the message that this was all right, this was manageable, this could be sustained; in case, dropping a single item from the terrible armful, they should feel the whole lot escaping from their grasp, and tumbling catastrophically down.

I didn't know this at the time. I was much too young to take in the causes and effects. I remember being asked which name I liked better, Bridget or Sophie, just after she was born; then nothing, just unmemorious early darkness, until a generic scene of all four of us in my parents' bed on a Sunday morning, me playing with a drift of red and white Lego pieces, Bridget already a year or so old, well into the routine of existing with a fingertip grasp on the medical precipice. What I knew, was that she went from being a small baby, to an emaciated child. Her legs dangled out of her frocks like strings. In her, the round family face we all shared became a neat little billiard ball very tightly stretched with skin, a sweet little death's-head. She could talk long before she could walk. The sugar water was the staple part of her diet, leaving her faintly nauseated a lot of the time, but it was important to tempt her to put aside the sick feeling, when she could, and to eat a little bit, a very little bit, of protein. My parents weighed out minuscule delicacies on a pair of white scales so small they would have made a more natural part of a drug dealer's equipment. "Look, Bridget," they said, "how about *a quarter of an ounce* of chicken?" They drafted Bridget's imaginary friend, Ben, and gave him a new passion for hiding the silver key to the sewing-machine case at the bottom of pipkins of cold milk; a key that would only be revealed if all the milk was drunk.

What I knew was that Bridget's fragility made the whole world fragile. It was compounded by my mother, in her early thirties, developing osteoporosis, the brittle-bone condition women don't usually get till after menopause. Bridget sat on rugs at family picnics, looking as if a breath of wind would blow her away; my mother sported ever-changing plaster casts as she collected fractures. Arm casts, leg casts, a complete upper-body cast. Whatever my life had been like before Bridget was born, it was over: cause for a sibling envy so big I didn't dare show it, or even *feel* it much, in case it cracked the thinned skeleton of what was left.

It hurt to look at Bridget's situation head-on, and I shied away from it. Consequently, although she was a familiar presence, I never really got to know her very well as an individual human proposition. Other people always praised her sense of humor. They seemed to see someone using a dry wit to cope. What wit, I thought? I never found her jokes funny. The ho-ho-ho-ing that greeted them struck me as forced; more than that, as a handy get-out for the people who laughed. It was like the famous put-down she had apparently come up with when I was six or so, and she was three, still rugbound, and entirely dependent on verbal comebacks. "You," she was supposed to have said, crushingly, "are a little piece of fluff"—and immediately this had been adopted into the family mythos as evidence that Bridget could take care of herself, oh yes. I distrusted it for that very reason. In truth, I don't know now whether her jokes were funny or not. I wish I could remember more of them. I dismissed them a priori, on principle. I could never believe in a self-possession large enough to encompass the ruin I perceived: therefore, she had none. I just saw raw vulnerability.

And ever since, I've hated vulnerable people. Bridget's mind worked just fine, until the very end, but for some reason it isn't the physically handicapped who remind me of her. People in wheelchairs seem reassuringly solid, somehow—anchored by gravity. It's the slow people, the learning disabled, the much euphemized fucked-of-wit I find unbearable, locked in their innocence, tottering through a world they don't understand in the misplaced confidence that it's safe. I remember seeing, on a

15

bus in London a couple of years ago, a girl of about twenty, not with Down's syndrome features, but with her head too small in proportion to her body, and a horribly hopeful smile. She had collected badges on her anorak. They weren't the cool kind memorializing bands or gigs or proudly weird teenage affiliations. They were crappy round ones two inches across, in lime green and custard yellow and Barbara Cartland pink, the sort you can buy on a wet morning in a seaside town from an overweight woman with a disfiguring goiter, operating a stall located where the pier and the human spirit both run out. They each had a joke on them in shaky black Letraset letters, SEX APPEAL: PLEASE GIVE GENEROUSLY and BEANS, BEANS ARE GOOD FOR YOUR HEART, THE MORE YOU EAT THE MORE YOU WHISTLE. She had unfunny jokes running right up one lapel and down the other; and the sight of her hurt my heart, and made my eyes prickle. I would have taken away what afflicted her if I could, but since I couldn't I hated her for what she made me feel, and I wished she was dead, or at any rate safely segregated somewhere where the sight of her didn't burrow at the long-buried roots in me of an intolerable pity: a pity I can't live up to, and can't bear to be reminded of.

So when I read stories obsessively as a child I was striking a kind of deal that allowed me to turn away. Sometime in childhood I made a bargain that limited, so I thought, the power over me that real experience had, the real experience that comes to us in act and incident and through the proximate, continuous existence of those we love. All right, I said, I'll let a quantity of *that* stream over me, if I can have a balancing portion of *this,* the other kind of experience, which is controlled, and repeatable, and comes off the page. I learned to pump up the artificial realities of fiction from page to mind at a pressure that equalized with the pressure of the world, so that (in theory) the moment I actually lived in could never fill me completely, whatever was happening. For the first years of the bargain, my idea was that good writing should vanish from attention altogether while you read it, so that the piped experience pressing back the world should seem as liquid and embracing—as unverbal—as what it competed with. Twenty-five years have gone by since then. My life has changed, and so has the content of my reading. But the bargain holds. Still, when I reach for a book, I am reaching for an equilibrium. I am reading to banish pity, and brittle bones. I am reading to evade guilt, and avoid consequences, and to limit time's hold on me: all thoughts far from prose. As far from prose as the obscure source of De Quincey's need was from laudanum.

Yet the substance must allow the addiction. Tobacco must deliver its hit of nicotine and its amazing bouquet of fragrant carcinogens, or no one could use it to allay nerves, or fend off sleep. The alkaloids of opium must have psychoactive properties when blood containing them reaches the brain, or De Quincey's history and De Quincey's need could not have fixed on them to structure his life from 1804 to 1859. And these potentials for addictiveness—which it takes an exterior motive to realize— contribute to our sense of what tobacco and opium *are*. Fiction too has qualities that permit it to be consumed as a drug: but they don't normally figure in the estimate of fiction's nature. They are the same qualities that give it its potential for revelation. They only have to be taken a little differently.

I began my reading in a kind of hopeful springtime for children's writing. I was born in 1964, so I grew up in a golden age comparable to the present heyday of J. K. Rowling and Philip Pullman, or to the great Edwardian decade when E. Nesbit,

Kipling, and Kenneth Grahame were all publishing at once. An equally amazing generation of talent was at work as the 1960s ended and the 1970s began. William Mayne was making dialogue sing; Peter Dickinson was writing the *Changes* trilogy; Alan Garner was reintroducing myth into the bloodstream of daily life; Jill Paton Walsh was showing that children's perceptions could be just as angular and uncompromising as those of adults; Joan Aiken had begun her Dido Twite series of comic fantasies; Penelope Farmer was being unearthly with *Charlotte Sometimes*; Diana Wynne Jones's gift for wild invention was hitting its stride; Rosemary Sutcliffe was just adding the final uprights to her colonnade of Romano-British historical novels; Leon Garfield was reinventing the eighteenth century as a scene for inky Gothic intrigue. The list went on, and on, and on. There was activity everywhere, a new potential classic every few months.

Unifying this lucky concurrence of good books, and making them seem for a while like contributions to a single intelligible project, was a kind of temporary cultural consensus: a consensus both about what children were and about where we all were in history. Dr. Spock's great manual for liberal, middle-class child-rearing had come out at the beginning of the sixties, and had helped deconstruct the last lingering remnants of the idea that a child was clay to be molded by benevolent adult authority. The new orthodoxy took it for granted that a child was a resourceful individual, neither ickily good nor reeking of original sin. And the wider world was seen as a place in which a permanent step forward toward enlightenment had taken place as well. The books my generation were offered took it for granted that poverty, disease, and prejudice essentially belonged in the past. Postwar society had ended them. As the 1970s went on, these assumptions would lose their credibility. Gender roles were about to be shaken up; the voices that a white, liberal consensus consigned to the margins of consciousness were about to be asserted as hostile witnesses to its nature. People were about to lose their certainty that liberal solutions worked. Evil would revert to being an unsolved problem. But it hadn't happened yet; and till it did, the collective gaze of children's stories swept confidently across past and future, and across all the international varieties of the progressive, orange-juice-drinking present, from Australia to Sweden, from Holland to the broad, clean suburbs of America.

For me, walking up the road aged seven or eight to spend my pocket money on a paperback, the outward sign of this unity was the dominance of Puffin Books. In Britain, almost everything written for children passed into the one paperback imprint. On the shelves of the children's section in a bookshop, practically all the stock would be identically neat soft-covered octavos, in different colors, with different cover art, but always with the same sans serif type on the spine, and the same little logo of an upstanding puffin. Everything cost about the same. For 17½p (about 45¢)—then 25p and then 40p as the 1970s inflation took hold—you could have any of the new books, or any of the children's classics, from the old ones like *The Wind in the Willows* or *Alice* to the ones that were only a couple of decades into their classichood, like the Narnia books. (C. S. Lewis had died the year before I was born, most unfairly making sure I would never meet him.) If you were a reading child in the UK in the sixties or the seventies, you too probably remember how securely authoritative Puffins seemed, with the long, trustworthy descriptions of the story inside the front cover, always written by the same arbiter, the Puffin editor Kaye Webb, and their astonishingly precise recommendation to "girls of eleven and above, and sensitive boys." It was as if Puffin were part of the administration of the world. They were the department of the welfare state responsible for the distribution of narrative. And their reach seemed universal: not just the really good books you were going to remember forever, but the nearly good ones too and the completely forgettable ones that at the time formed the wings of reading and spread them wide enough to enfold you in books on all sides. They provided us with Romans, Vikings, knights and squires, Elizabethan adventurers and lonely Victorians. They showed us ruined futures and gleaming ones, magical alternative worlds and frightening ones. They conducted us through adventures happening right now to capable kids everywhere, all building tree houses or thwarting criminals or engaging in off-the-wall badinage with cranky-but-witty old ladies. Or separated from adults by earthquake or air crash, and surviving; the same squabbles between kids as when playing proving here to produce good adaptable decisions to build a signal fire, to loot abandoned shops for canned food, to find a way across a river. Or generally just darting early, early out of the house to meet the gang on the first day of the holidays, after a breakfast eaten under protest, the bright world beckoning, the tall grasses hissing against the bike wheels.

It would be nice to think that my reading only gained its glint of desperation when I crossed the boundary out of this hopeful domain. But memory tells me that it wasn't so. I know that at ten I could already hold an Arthur Ransome story about sailing on the Norfolk Broads just as tightly in my mind's grip as I squeezed any of the words I read later about gushing intestines, or about sex. The passion aroused by fiction can be for any of the things that are absent at the time of reading; any greedy wish will do. The adventure with jibbooms and bobstays triggered no hormonal cascade in me, as some of the things I read nowadays certainly do, but I felt the downrush of an earlier kind of resolving intensity. My reaction to the deployments of story *itself* was fierce.

I knew that I needed to start at the beginning. So I have gone back and read again the sequence of books that carried me from babyhood to the age of nineteen, from the first fragmentary stories I remember to the science fiction I was reading on the brink of adulthood. As I reread them, I tried to become again the reader I had been when I encountered each for the first time, wanting to know how my particular history, in my particular family, at that particular time, had ended up making me into the reader I am today. I made forays into child psychology, philosophy, and psychoanalysis, where I thought those things might tease out the implications of memory. With their help, the following chapters recount a path through the riches that were available to the children of the 1960s and 1970s, and onward into the reading of adolescence. It is the story (I hope) of the reading my whole generation of bookworms did; and it is the story of my own relationship with books; both. A pattern emerged, or I drew it: a set of four stages in the development of that space inside where writing is welcomed and reading happens. What follows is more about books than it is about me, but nonetheless it is my inward autobiography, for the words we take into ourselves help to shape us. They help form the questions we think are worth asking; they shift around the boundaries of the sayable inside us, and the related borders of what's acceptable; their potent images, calling on more in us than the responses we will ourselves to have, dart new bridges into being between our conscious and unconscious minds, between what we know we know, and the knowledge we cannot examine by thinking. They build and stretch and build again the chambers of our imagination.

In the meantime a child is sitting reading. Between the black lines of print and the eye, a channel is open, up which information is pouring; more and faster than in any phone call, or any micro-coded burst of data fired across the Net either, if you consider that these signals are not a sequence of numbers, not variations on a limited set of digital possibilities, but item after item of news from the analogue world of perception, each infinitely inflectable in tone and intent. The prince sighs as his sick horse refuses to take sugar from his hand. Oatmeal sky over dank heather. It is a truth universally acknowledged that a man in possession of a fortune must be in want of a wife. Engage the star drive! Yet the receiving mind files away impression after impression after impression. (Sometimes, to be sure, only in a mental container marked DON'T GET IT.) This heterogeneous traffic leaves no outward trace. You cannot tell what is going on by looking at it: the child just sits there, with her book or his. It cannot be overheard, makes no incomprehensible chittering like the sound of a modem working on a telephone line. The subtlest microphone lowered into the line of the transmission will detect nothing, retrieve nothing, from that incalculable flow of images.

CHAPTER TWO

The Forest

■ ■ ■

At the beginning of my life, there was a forest. I grew up in a staff house on the campus of Keele University, surrounded by institutional concrete. Occasionally the fantastical qualities of the times showed themselves. In 1968 the students all took their clothes off to protest the Vietnam War. Two students who baby-sat me painted a map of Middle Earth across an entire wall of their lodgings. Rumor had it that a Tolkien-loving academic gave a lecture in Elvish. Across the road from our front door, though, the Keele woods began. They were the plantations of an eighteenth-century park that had run wild during the neglectful reign of Keele's last squire, and never been completely taken in hand again once they'd passed into the cash-strapped public sector. What had been designed as a grand garden of many different botanical moods—like a cabinet with many different drawers—was shaggy now, overgrown and intergrown. Species had crept; the seams between Capability Brown's separate ideas had closed; the cells of the wood had knitted together. Yet the design remained, fuzzily, because the woods contained many zones, samples of different kinds of forest close together in space but far apart in spirit. I didn't know the names of the trees—I still don't, mostly—but there was an area where broad, resinous black-green pines kept the ground shadowed and bare, and the turning path was carpeted with dry needles and fir cones; a stand of high beeches whose elephant-hide bark rose out of drifts of small gold leaves like coins; a neat conical hill that had been colonized by yellow and green sycamore saplings. There were oceans of shiny-leaved rhododendrons, which I'd crash into deliberately on my bike later, so that I somersaulted over the handlebars and disappeared into the branches in an explosion of pink petals. There was a dark zone dominated by alders around a stagnant pool, some kind of folly once, like the sandstone amphitheater elsewhere in the woods, but given over now to algae and leaf mold.

There was a forest at the beginning of fiction too. This one spread forever. Its canopy of branches covered the land, covered every form of the land, whether the ground beneath jagged or rolled. The forest went on. Up in its living roof birds flitted through greenness and bright air, but down between the trunks of the many trees there were shadows, there was dark. When you walked this forest your feet made rustling sounds, but the noises you made yourself were not the only noises, oh no. Twigs snapped; breezes brought snatches of what might be voices. Lumpings and crashes in the undergrowth marked the passages of heavy things far off, or suddenly nearby. This was a populated wood. All wild creatures lived here, dangerous or benign according to their natures. And all the other travelers you had heard of were in the wood too, at this very moment: kings and knights, youngest sons and third daughters, simpletons and outlaws; a small girl whose bright hood flickered between the pine trees like a scarlet beacon, and a wolf moving on a different vector to intercept her at the cottage, purposefully arrowing through thickets, leaving a track of disturbance behind him as an alpha particle does when it streaks across a cloud chamber. These people, these dangers were not far away, but you would never meet them. The adventures could never intersect, although they shared the forest; although they would be joined in time by more, and still more, wayfarers, the more elaborated beings who came from the more elaborate worlds of privately read story, rather than the primitives of fairy tale. Mole from *The Wind in the Willows* would pelt in hunted panic through a nighttime tract of the forest, whose bare boughs jutted "like a black reef in some still southern sea." Through twisted foliage would creep the Wart, in *The Sword in the Stone,* past pale-eyed predators and baby dragons hissing under stones, to his first sight of Merlyn swearing at a bucket. But each traveled separately, because it was the nature of the forest that you were alone in it. It was the place in which by definition you had no companions, and no resources except your own uncertain self. It was the Wild, where relationship ceases, where connection is suspended. There would be encounters, of course. Eventually the state that the whole wood represented would be embodied. One of those rustlings would become a footfall, would become a meeting, and you stepped forward to it as best you could. You could no more avoid the encounters of the wood—all significant, all in their way tests—than you could cross it on a neat dependable path. It existed to cause changes, and it had no pattern you could take hold of in the hope of evading change. You never came out the same as when you went in. Here and again, an old tree had fallen, and a dozen saplings were competing for its access to the sky. Depending on which succeeded, that unit of woodland space would be colored one particular green out of a dozen possibilities. The forest had been made by a million events equally lacking in intention. It was rich and it was strange: mile after mile, a carpet without a design.

And there was a forest at the beginning of history. The summerhouse in Cambridge where I sit writing this and watching a sycamore throw down its dry leaves one by one, stands on what was once the marshland edge of a wood as total as the forest of story. The botanist Oliver Rackham called it the "wildwood" as a technical term, after Kenneth Grahame's Wild Wood. I sit in the ghost of the wildwood's Lime Province, a wonderful name, the title for a polity of trees alone. It stretched from sea to sea. Painted people slipped through its shadows, among the other animal species of the wildwood, indistinct in the slatted light. They left no permanent trails. They hunted and gathered, they retreated to basketwork houses where lakes had opened the land for them. Undoubtedly they told stories about the unending thicket whose signs they forever tried to read.

But those stories are lost. From the picture books of history I read in the early seventies I learned a version of the British past in which the wildwood endured into the Middle Ages, to be the Old English Jungle the Wart got lost in. Then men wearing hoods and woolly tights grubbed up the trees. It was a traditional history that produced an almost moralized contrast between the wild and the tame, and it fitted the fortunes of the landscape neatly together with the characteristics of the different inhabitants of the country. I had a vivid picture in my head of dead-straight Roman roads cleaving through endless green, joining square little white cities in clearings; and another image for what happened when the Saxons came and overthrew all the neat diagrams that made up Roman civilization. I saw trees sprouting back through the roofs of smashed villas. The mosaics bubbled like boiling water as the tree roots writhed under them, and spilled into fragments lost in the undergrowth. In other moods I knew the forest was the domain of magic, and I was sorry it had been lost, I was on the forest's side. I wanted the place under the leaves that had never been owned or designed, where everything might happen that had withdrawn from the tamed landscape of the present. But the Saxons represented a fearful disorder. They were wreckers, they were the enemies of all exact lines and reliable shapes. They were chaos. When the wildwood was their ally it seemed purely fearsome.

However, while I was imagining this vegetable holocaust circa 1972, Rackham and other investigators were using pollen analysis and archaeological data to displace the chronology it depended on. Roman Britain and Saxon Britain were both, in fact, cleared landscapes. Woods coppiced for firewood and building poles stood amid open fields. The wildwood had arrived at the close of the last Ice Age, around 11,000 B.C., reached its climax state about 4000 B.C., and began to be whittled back as soon as the Mesolithic discovery of agriculture reached Britain. By 2000 B.C. there were big open spaces on the chalk uplands; by 500 B.C. half the wildwood had gone and a rising population with axes in their hands were constantly forcing up the clearance rate. The significance of these dates is that they put the death of the British wildwood before recorded memory. Memory in the forms of history or chronicle we could be without, and still inherit the shadow of the trees. But the death of the wildwood precedes story too; it happened before the oldest legends that now survive were first told. It is out of legend's reach. For stories to descend from then till now, there has to be a chain of peoples passing along mythology. They garble it, they subject it to the chaotic changes of Chinese Whispers, like the Celts of the second century B.C. who copied copies of Greek money till the chariot on the back disintegrated into a fluid whirl of dots and lines. Still, a signal arrives. Stories do not lapse easily into time's white noise because they are not passed on passively. There's a counterchaotic imperative at work. Whenever static threatens to overwhelm them, whenever too much detail becomes meaningless, a teller will reform them in the act of transmission so that once more they make (a kind of) contemporary sense. But the wildwood predates the earliest, obscurest functioning link in the chain. It sends us no signal at all. It was just too long ago. We tell no stories of the great wood from memory in England.

Instead, we narrate it in the same spirit that the Hopi Indians of the American Southwest tell tales hinging on orphans being cruelly abandoned in the wilderness. There are no orphans in traditional Hopi society. It would be culturally impossible for a child to fall right through their densely failsafed weave of family, no matter who died. If there was no father or mother, there would be an aunt; if there were no aunts or uncles, there would be a cousin; if there were no cousins, there would still be someone. But even for Hopis, the *situation* of abandonment seems to be a necessary one to imagine, to hug to oneself in the form of a story. It focuses a self-pity that everyone wants to feel sometimes, and that perhaps helps a child or an adolescent to think through their fundamental separateness. The situation expresses the solitude humans discover as we grow up no matter how well our kinship systems work.

The forest is necessary in the same way, whether or not real woodland figures much in the daily experience of those telling stories. Some of Britain's most famous forest tales are imports from more wooded cultures: "Hansel and Gretel" and "Little Red Riding Hood" were molded by the real landscapes of Germany and France respectively. When they traveled across the Atlantic with the English-speaking settlers of America, they were re-introduced into an environment where actual forests gave a daily corollary to the tales. But even in England it made sense to tell them, despite Rackham's anti-magical discovery that by the time of the Domesday Book in 1086 it would already have been impossible for Hansel and Gretel to walk more than four miles through any English wood in any direction without burst-ing back out into open fields. The trail of white pebbles would really not have been required. With real forests or without them, we tell the story regardless, knowing that when the lost children recede through deep after deep of the trees, they are plumbing a different geography. They are journeying into the deep spaces of myth, which does not demand a location, only a vivid referent—a tree line imprinted onto the imagination.

Like the desert or the mountain where the Hopi child struggles, the forest too is concerned with solitude; the forest too symbolizes the place in which the traveler must realize his separateness. "In many European fairy tales," wrote Bruno Bettelheim, "the brother who leaves soon finds himself in a deep, dark forest, where he feels lost, having given up the orga-nization of his life which the parental home provided, and not yet having built up the inner structures which we develop only under the impact of life experiences we have to master more or less on our own." So far so similar. But the forest has other, particular qualities. It's *thick* wilderness. You cannot see far through it: it thwarts perception. It's a place of formless impres-sions you must somehow understand, of aboriginal darkness and confusion. No one in a story was ever taken to a forest and offered all the kingdoms of the earth, or invited to turn stones into bread. Jesus was being tempted on the mountaintop and in the desert to show *mastery,* and empty sands or gulfs of air are sites that challenge the traveler's powers, divine or otherwise. But the forest is where you are when your surroundings are not mastered. In the psychoanalytic tradition the forest is therefore identified as the great symbol of the unconscious. "The dark, hidden, near-impenetrable world of our unconscious," said Bettelheim, in his psychoanalyst's account of the fairy tale, *The Uses of Enchantment.* It is the mind's necessary wilderness. It is entwined because its separate growths have never been distinguished or uttered. It is dark because the fears and desires that grow here have not been admitted to the light of awareness. And it is trackless, because you never visit here in the state of conscious attention needed for pathfinding—unless, says the tradition, you make the analytical journey, take the couch trip under the sky of leaves, with its special dialectic of understanding between patient and therapist.

Strict, antique psychoanalytical thinking would leave it at that, privileging only the one science (or art) of discovery. Dreams carry you there, but they bring you the classically unconscious access to *the* unconscious, a night ride to the forest that plunges you down through its canopy, hurtles you through its thickets of material as if the Wild Hunt were at your heels (and perhaps they are, it depends what you're dreaming). Stories were once viewed by Freudians as doing essentially dreamlike things with their unconscious content: they were valuable as reservoirs of pattern and insight, but they were documents to which the explanatory system of psychoanalysis had to be brought. Freud praised writers for knowing intuitively what analysts studied laboriously, a judgment that, if you think about it, comes precious close to complimenting writers on having natural rhythm. So stories were too much *of* the forest to orient you in it. But, first tentatively, then with accelerating fervor, the active and shaping powers of story began to be conceded. Stories were admitted as conscious instruments to handle the unconscious, in sync with a humbler perception of psychoanalysis itself as producing a kind of story from the interplay in the consulting room.

They've now come to be seen as deliberate journeys to the forest, which may enable self-knowledge all the more profound because they speak directly, in the mind's own rich language of symbols. They have shifted from the problem to the solution side of the ledger. Bettelheim himself pointed out, "A fairy tale is not a neurotic symptom": you are not trying to dissect it to make it go away. He described the ancient Indian practice of prescribing a story to the troubled in mind, for them to sift and contemplate. That was 1975. His endorsement of stories as therapeutic made him a pioneer. Since then, a crowd has followed him, offering all the deliberately crafted "myths" of pop-psych self-help: Iron John, the Woman Who Runs with the Wolves, the promotion of the tarot pack as a "box of stories" tailored to individual needs. Whether this cultural move is an overcompensation for the previous error depends on whether stories are truly benign just because they are potent in their operation on the psyche, whether they are guides to the forest just because they give powerful commentary on it.

Different schools of therapy of course produce different forests. The Freudian unconscious, therefore the Freudian forest, is a firmly individual affair. It contains only those unacknowledged fears and desires that our own life has laid down there. It's a private wood, growing differently in everybody. Jung's collective unconscious, on the other hand, provides a shared forest. A million separate paths lead into the one terrain.

Then, we don't just tell parallel stories, or dream similar dreams. We tap an elemental experience: an idea verging on mysticism or magic if you let it be more than a metaphor. The place, of course, in which such a metaphor can become concrete less problematically is—in a story, for fictional magic does not amount to a claim for magic's reality. One of the best English writers working in fantasy now has used the Jungian forest to circumvent the post-Rackham chronology for the English landscape. Robert Holdstock's Ryhope Wood reconciles everyday and mythic geographies by being, like the Tardis, bigger on the inside than the outside. To look at from the plowed land beyond its boundaries, it is a modest mixed-oak stand of trees. Find the way in—read the leaf-sign and the earth-sign aright—and its boughs become green arches over a territory of wonder and horror that extends backward and backward and backward into the past. You have found the door to the wildwood. As you journey inward, you descend a well of time that distends the landscape just as a gravity well stretches space. The further in you go, the stranger grow the people of the wood, the remoter the mythology from which they come, until they far precede memory. At Ryhope's impassable center the Ice Age comes into view. Yet the outlaws and the tribes, the shamans and the monsters, unknown though they are, remain familiar. Ryhope is populated by every mythic figure ever placed in the forest, whether or not they are consciously remembered. The wood's responsive; it's a field of force, acted on by minds beyond its perimeter. It vivifies thought. Only, what comes alive in Ryhope, alive and dangerous, is the Jungian collective unconscious, a complete history of our species' time beneath the trees, coiled unnoticed in our brainstems. "Did she form out of the leaf-litter? Did wild animals carry sticks together and shape them into bones, and then, over the autumn, dying leaves fall and coat the bones in wildwood flesh? Was there a moment, in the wood, when something approximating to a human creature rose from the underbrush, and was shaped to perfection by the intensity of the human will, operating outside the woodland?"

It is good to know that real woods, even in England, hold very small areas that may not have changed since the wildwood. In leg-breaking gullies, on precipitous slopes, there are reservoirs of ancient vegetation perhaps a few feet square that have never been cleared. From here, lime seedlings or snake's-head fritillaries replenish the wood around. These too are doors.

If the forest is where we go when, in Bettelheim's words, we "lose the framework which gave structure to our past life," we can go there at any age. Any time can be the time when structure collapses and the tangle of roots and branches surrounds us. The order we are living by ends without warning or after long struggle, it crashes or it dies of exhaustion. And for the third or fifth or umpteenth time the leaves are under our feet again. "In the middle of the journey of this life, I was traveling through a dark wood," begins the *Divine Comedy*. Dante's neat balance on a medieval life's midpoint makes him thirty. From the dark wood hell gapes, heaven beckons, purgatory promises refining fire. But however many times we return, there's a first time for the forest. It is also the place we begin, as individuals: which perhaps explains the permanent temptation to line up childhood and primitiveness together, to try and combine the early time of one human and of a society. It is the place a baby is, before the developing mind has built up a model of things that it can rely on. It is the place we are before structure. Before we master speech, and can wield the power of names to distinguish the elements of the world—before we know for sure that our self has a boundary, and does not exist in a warm, milky continuum with everything else—we are in the forest. We don't so much enter the wood as find ourselves there: knowing a little more that it *is* a wood, in fact, with each success at naming and placing. Gradually we recognize the dark uprights around us as trees. This first time, the forest doesn't represent an emotional state. Dante's dark wood is grown of emotions not disentangled, a spiritual state not articulated in the literal sense of not being split into the separate, hinged units of feeling that make us able to take the sad compound conditions of adulthood in a train, in a sequence, and so understand them. But for the infant coming to him- or herself in the wood for the first time, the problem is cognitive. Think of the cross sections through the brain that a medical scanner produces: those false-color images of activity, red and violet, yellow and orange. They map a greenwood inside our heads. When we're born there are few paths established yet; the dendrites linking our neurons are a random tangle; the world is all to learn. From this forest, stories help to lead us out. The first stories we encounter, that is. The fragmentary sequences that first make a wavering, storylike sense, like the "story" of a letter arriving through a letterbox. The stories in picture books read aloud to one-year-olds and two-year-olds. Eventually, the fairy tales, which themselves are spiky with pine needles.

The only accounts of very young children are given by adults observing them. Not only can a child of one not speak to describe the time before language: they can't remember it when they have become adults of thirty. Usually a person's earliest memories go back to when they were three or four. Memory development is closely linked to language development. Not all memories are verbal—some of the most potent are gestalts of color and mood that would be completely irreducible to words—but the ability to store absent sensation calls on the same faculties as the ability to represent the world in symbolic form. So the knowledge of the prelinguistic forest has all been arrived at by adults working like anthropologists. They look at the strange tribe of infants, and try to deduce an inward order from the behavior that they can see.

The scope for fantasy on the adult's part is great. In *Through the Looking Glass* Alice enters "the wood . . . where things have no names." She meets a Fawn. Without names, neither knows what they are.

> So they walked on together through the wood, Alice with her arms clasped lovingly round the soft neck of the Fawn, till they came out into another open field, and here the Fawn gave a sudden bound into the air, and shook itself free from Alice's arm. "I'm a Fawn!" it cried out in a voice of delight. "And, dear me! you're a human child!" A sudden look of alarm came into its beautiful brown eyes, and in another moment it had darted away at full speed.

Anyone who has ever seen an eighteen-month-old in pursuit of a house cat knows that the real forest of unknowing is not the peaceable kingdom where the lion lies down with the lamb. Lewis Carroll was seduced by the adult wish for an alternative to the cynicism of adult self-consciousness. He describes, with cynicism and amusement, a place where there is neither, because in the absence of words everything is at rest. As a fantasy that reverses a fall it has a lot in common with Peter Pan. But early childhood is not a stable surface on which to project the dream of innocence—any more than later childhood can be fixed comfortably at a stage from which a real child would want never to grow up. The only child who never grows up is the child that adults imagine themselves being. A real child perpetually changes, has new experiences, has the same experiences in new ways; constantly moves on; declares that they are a subject in their own right. And the forest before language is neither innocent nor silent. A toddler who has not yet spoken, or a baby who has not yet walked, is still reaching and receiving, ceaselessly sorting out the world, in physical ways that are also cognitive explorations. There is no point of origin for human beings, if by that we mean some stationary moment at which nothing is going on. From the moment when the fertilized cell starts dividing, there is always something going on.

Jean Piaget, who was the great modern pioneer explorer of the purposefulness of young children, also insisted on the radical difference of their minds. After the first era of life when all knowledge is body knowledge—the "sensory-motor period" in his terminology—a child who has discovered speech becomes "preoperational." Preoperational children, he concluded from his work in the 1920s and 1930s on Swiss three- and four-year-olds, see the world in some distinctive ways. They are egocentric, for example, as revealed in the common belief that the sun and moon follow them when they go for a walk. They think that almost everything that moves is alive including clouds and cars, only gradually restricting life to those things that move of their own accord. (There's an exception: right from the start, anything broken is dead.) Conversely, they believe that the natural world was all arranged as it is for human benefit—was artificially constructed to suit. A large part of the preschool population of Geneva, it turned out, thought that Lake Geneva had been dug deliberately after the city was built, by men with spades. All these "distortions," put together, make up a world neither coldly material nor alive with a life that is going about its own business indifferent to the child, but instead magically responsive, surrounding the child at its center like the ring of painting on the inside of a zoetrope. But underlying these elaborate beliefs, Piaget argued, were difficulties in grasping reality's elementary truths, the most basic laws governing the behavior of things. The magical aspects of the world of a three-year-old did not present a fundamental challenge to the adult understanding. But these differences in perception down at the roots almost defied imagination.

It is a law of the world for adults that the physical properties of the environment around you change only in predictable ways, by predictable processes (barring events arriving from completely outside the ordinary context of things, such as meteor strikes or earthquakes). For adults, the world is dynamic, but intelligible, at least at the level of everyday sense-perception. Preoperational children, according to Piaget's experiments, seemed not to know that things existed in dependable quantities. They had learned to recognize that an object kept its identity even when its appearance changed, so Daddy in a hat was still Daddy: that was one of the cognitive achievements they needed to graduate from the sensory-motor period. But they weren't out of the woods yet. They didn't yet know that physical attributes were also "conserved," so that if the attributes changed, there was always compensation for a shrinking in one dimension by growth in another. Show a preop child a row of buttons, then spread them out and the child would say that now there were more of them. Line up two identical wooden rods, and the child would agree they were the same length. Slide the lower one to the left, and suddenly to the child it became "longer." Roll a ball of modeling clay out into a sausage, and Presto! It was "bigger."

It's difficult to remember thinking like this, because as the child learns to conserve the different attributes of material things, in a predictable sequence leading up to the conservation of volume, which is hardest of all, each item once mastered becomes natural and inevitable, and impossible to un-know again. These are the "operations" a child must master in Piaget's model, before moving on to the next stage of development at six or seven: the traditional age of reason in many cultures, he noted. The operations were procedures of logic, but not as in mathematical logic. They were logic's atoms, its ground rules from which all else followed; its simplest moves, that let you deal with the changing world by knowing that if A is bigger than B, B must be smaller than A.

One of Piaget's most famous experiments was designed to demonstrate the preop child's inability to handle another of the operations, "class inclusion." Class inclusion is when one category of things nests entirely within a larger category of things. The class of "women," for example, fits *inside* the class of "people." The problem is to understand the relationship between part and whole. Piaget tested it with beads. He laid out a row of (say) nine brown and three white beads—enough for the imbalance between the two colors to be immediately strik-ing. Then he asked: "Are there more beads, or more brown beads?" Virtually without exception, preoperational children replied that there were more brown beads. The older his test subjects were, and the closer they had come to the next era in their development, the more troubling they found the test, the more aware they were that something was awry, though they couldn't put their finger on it. Piaget took this as proof that a child younger than six or seven is cognitively incapable of relating a whole to its parts. If this is true, it is not a trivial point of logic. Knowing how to fit phenomena into categories of different sizes is as fundamental to understanding the world as being able to tell what is bigger and what is smaller. It isn't a question of young children not being able to say that a whole is greater than a part. This is about them not even being able to know so. If Piaget was right, the child who listens to a fairy tale doesn't know there is more weather than there is sunshine, more pets than there are cats, more cutlery than there are spoons. If Piaget was right, then the magical forest in which a three-year-old will find it natural for animals to speak is very dense indeed; is a thicket; because the child literally cannot tell the trees from the wood, the wood from the trees.

As a set of metaphors, Piaget's sequence of stages is unquestionably valuable. That's how I use them throughout this book: his progression from preoperative thought, to concrete operations, to abstract operations, gave me a loose conceptual map for my whole history as a reader. But for the last twenty or thirty years developmental psychologists have increasingly challenged Piaget on such crucial details as the class-inclusion problem, and their disagreement focuses on language. For a start, "Are there more beads, or more brown beads?" is a question that could well catch out an adult, without implying that they hadn't mastered class inclusion. For Piaget, the only difficulty of the sentence is the underlying cognitive difficulty. To understand it correctly requires you to notice that "beads" and "brown beads" belong on different levels in a ladder of categories, which is what Piaget intended. But it also requires you to discount, or override, the very strong expectation set up by the form of the sentence itself that you are going to be comparing parallel categories of things, that is, categories on the same level of the ladder. Children who get Piaget's question wrong are clearly behaving as if he had asked a more natural question, one that goes with the grain of an "Are there ... or are there ..." question, rather than against it. They are telling him whether there are more brown beads or *white* ones. Recent psychologists are not as comfortable as Piaget was with this deceptive linguistic cue.

More fundamentally, they disagree over the role language itself plays in the mind's development. Piaget thought that language only tracked the growth of understanding. In the Piagetian system, spoken language was the great achievement of the first two years of life, and by letting the child manipulate the world through a set of shared symbols, it immensely accelerated learning in every other area, so in that sense it was deeply implicated in every later achievement. But Piaget took it as common sense that a child learned something first, then was able to say it. Words expressed what you already knew. They didn't contribute on their own account—or lead intellectual development in particular directions. If this were true, if language were transparent like this, then the form in which the bead question was cast (barring obvious difficulties of vocabulary) should not make any difference to whether a preoperational child could answer it. In the early 1970s James McGarrigle set out to experiment with multiple versions of the class-inclusion problem, some altering the wording, some changing the other attributes of the test that might strike a child. He discovered straightaway that you could increase significantly the number of children who got the test right if you put in an extra adjective drawing attention to what the whole class had in common, as opposed to its black/white subsections. Lay out toy cows lying down, and ask if there were more black cows or more *sleeping* cows, and the proportion of right answers almost doubled. He also discovered—a finding that goes beyond the role of language but bears vitally on it—that the more the wording and the other aspects of the test were adjusted together to make the situation familiar, and the clearer the intention of the adult asking the question consequently grew to the children, the more able they were to direct their minds to the right contrast—black/total rather than black/white. Young children could pass the class-inclusion test if it was presented to them in particular ways; which proved that they were not defeated by the part-whole relationship down at its cognitive root, with the bizarre consequences for their inner worlds implied by Piaget, because that kind of complete inability would not have been altered by any alterations in the testing. What they could *not* do, it seemed, was easily comprehend the kind of language represented by "Are there more beads, or more brown beads?"

McGarrigle's colleague Margaret Donaldson, whose *Children's Minds* became one of the most important statements of the revisionist case, pointed out that to answer Piaget's original question a child had to ignore a set of things. They would have to ignore their own sense of what question it was probable you would ask about some white beads and some brown ones; and overlook the familiar sentence haunting the unfamiliar sentence that the questioner actually spoke; and reject any instinctive guess about what the questioner's intention was likely to be. In short, the child had to ignore every piece of data except the exact wording of the question. This proved to be the very hardest thing for children to do. The work of Donaldson, McGarrigle, and many others showed that small children understood language best when it was, so to speak, fused with a situation, and all the nonlinguistic clues to hand could be brought to bear. They called this "embedded" language; it is speech "embedded . . . in the flow of events which accompany it." An example would be an adult saying "Come here" while beckoning and smiling. A child would have to be very young, just on the cusp of articulate speech, to need nonverbal clues in that instance, but even in adulthood whether speech is embedded continues to affect how easy it is to understand. A proposition in the abstract terms of logic becomes strikingly easier for most people to follow once it is translated into words that refer to natural, concrete situations—although the conceptual content remains the same.

This permanent inclination in humans to grasp words quicker when events sustain them directs us back to a time when words and events ran much closer together in our minds, and we were "reading" what happened around us without making hard-and-fast distinctions between what people said and what it seemed they wanted. To rip a question completely out of its context, and to consider it purely as a mechanism of words interacting to produce one precise meaning, requires a three-year-old or a four-year-old to go against this whole current in the mind. It is either very difficult, or actually impossible. "The child is not able to pay scrupulous attention to the language in its own right," concluded Donaldson. She pointed out that in the extreme case, if they've come from a family where they're never encouraged to play with the spoken language, it is possible for preschool children not even to know that separate words are what they are speaking. They can perceive language as a flow, a continuum, instead of a succession of units. Of course, the word as a unit is intrinsic to speech: our ability to talk at all, at any age, is dependent on a mental grammar that splits up our thoughts into distinct chunks of meaning that play different

grammatical roles. But the process can be completely unconscious for a small child, since the last stage of utterance for a
human being—the part you actually notice—is the further conversion of the grammatical string into sounds that do indeed
flow continuously from throat, tongue, and lips. We float our
words on "a river of breath," as one scholar of linguistics put it,
and we leave no audible spaces between them. So it may only be
the river that a child hears.

In place of Piaget's breakthrough into recognizable, "opera-
tional" rationality at the age of six or seven, the revisionists
saw a parallel achievement, in language. Piaget's bead question,
it was clear, did measure something significant. When children
reached the point of being able to answer it in its original,
tricksy form, something had changed, a new stage of development had been reached. But the ability that had arrived then
was the ability to perceive language as a system with formal
rules dictating what a sentence must mean, even if the meaning
went dead against expectations. The ability to handle the
underlying logic had arrived years earlier, the flow of words
helping to thin the internal trees long before the child could
formulate the abstract relationship between a tree and a wood.

The reliance on embedded language isn't a weakness in
small children. On the contrary: it is the first way that language
becomes powerful for them, as a tool in their understanding of
the world. It's limited, but it's primary. Through it they can
grasp far more than Piaget imagined. They judge, assess, combine, and conserve much earlier than he supposed; they slot
objects into groups, and groups into bigger groups. They cannot
be as egocentric as he deduced they were, if they spend their
time tracking the likely intentions of other people around
them, sometimes to the detriment of exact comprehension of

difficult statements. It is not just that they cannot easily pay close attention to language that is not embedded. It is that they can pay the closest attention of their lives so far to embedded language.

And what, paradoxically, is the most embedded form of language, for all that it seems devoted to carrying those who hear it outside the context of the moment? What way of speaking deals out situations one after another, is full of concrete particulars, and keeps a beady eye on people's intentions all the time? What packs in cognitive material most richly into a form children are able to attend to? The story. Arthur Applebee, studying children's response to stories in the 1970s, discovered that around 70 percent of two-year-olds have already begun to use the conventions which tell you that a certain piece of speech is a story, and not some other kind of remark, or joke, or instruction. The special past tense of stories usually comes first, followed by the discovery of the special opening formulas that inform a listener they should now transfer their gaze to happenings entirely sustained by words. Once upon a time. Long ago and faraway. When the people were animals and the animals were people. In the olden days . . .

Meanwhile, from the very earliest stages of language acquisition, the child is learning to take words sensuously as well as functionally, for it is the structures of meaning that she or he cannot be scrupulously aware of, not language's texture, its timbre, its grain—all gloriously embedded things. Rhythm precedes words altogether; the faculty for rhyme grows faster than the vocabulary of words to rhyme *with,* and spills over into nonsense. Ran, gan, splan, tran, pan, blan. Or there's the pleasure in the music of lines where only a word in ten is yet understood. "Mister Magnolia has only one boot / He has two lovely sisters who play on the flute / And his dinosaur, what a magnificent brute!" "I do not like green eggs and ham / I do not like them, Sam-I-Am." Who cares what a dinosaur is, whether eggs can be green. Sounds make subtle patterns. In 1962 the psychologist Ruth Weir noted that her son Anthony, twenty-eight months old, was repeating "lipstick like a blanket" over and over in his cot before sleep: not just making an analogy between the lipstick his mother put to her mouth and the blanket he was holding to his, but building an intensely satisfying trio of lines in which the *l* sound was followed by the *k* sound:

*L*ipstic*k*
*l*i*k*e a
b*l*an*k*et

—all setting up the pulse that beats on through one strand of language to the most developed and complex rhythmic achievements; to

Of Man's first Disobedience, and the Fruit of that Forbidden Tree . . .

And the stories begin.

But then we are a storytelling species. The biologist Steven Pinker has argued that there is an evolutionary advantage in a language arranged so that it aids prediction of what is going to happen next in a world of potential food and potential danger. Across the whole species, all human languages seize that advantage by naming phenomena as objects or actions, nouns or verbs. This fundamental decision allows humans to construct the flexible, intensely useful sequences of words that tell us who did what, what went where—what is going on. There were other logical possibilities for language, Pinker shows: the logician W. V. Quine has explored some of them. We might have distributed the properties of nouns and of verbs between several different kinds of hybrid words, meaning a-thing-and-its-motion or maybe a-thing-and-its-surroundings. Because we didn't, our language has a structural bias toward expressions that stay on the same level of reference: another reason why Piaget's bead question is intrinsically hard to understand. There just aren't any naturally occurring terms meaning a-thing-and-its-category. And because we went for nouns and verbs as the building blocks, every sentence is a model of an event. It's a report; or we could say, just as truly, that it's a story. From this point of view, it hardly matters whether the event is real or imaginary. The essential breakthrough of human language is that events of every kind are *represented*. We tell stories all the time when we speak. Storytelling may be the function that made language worth acquiring. The two-year-old who has started to understand the rules of story is coming into an inheritance that may be as genetic as the upright gait of our branch of primates, or our opposable thumbs.

What first teaches us the nature of story is not the fixed form of writing on a page. It isn't the page that teaches us that story is language miraculously fixed into an unvarying shape, which makes absent things present, as if the common air had stilled in its place and become hard crystal, through which you see visions. That comes after. The medium of the first encounter is an adult voice speaking, and saying the same words in the same order each time the story comes around. Once a small child grasps the principle, no one is more eager for the repetition to be exact. The words have to be right, or they aren't *the story*. "Don't say 'The fox met a family of ducks.' Say: "The fox met *Mr. and Mrs. Duck and all their duckling children!*'" The invariability of a story is what gives it a secure existence. It adds it to the expanding sphere of what is known for sure; and therefore to the dependable world, which is made up at the deepest level, for a small child, of patterns on which it is safe to rely. Piaget called the patterns in an infant's head "schemes." They begin very simple. There is one scheme of "everything that will go into my mouth." Then it subdivides, and there are separate schemes for food and for not-food. Complexity mounts up. Another way of seeing it is to say that small children agree intuitively with Wittgenstein. "The world is the totality of facts, not of things." It's what you know to be true that constitutes the world. Objects are terribly important, but the things in the small child's world that she or he can touch—the red brick that somehow encapsulates the nature of the whole box of bricks, the kitchen furniture nested at the center of the whole geography of home—count just as one type of true fact. Objects are just a subset of a scheme that has already divided, the scheme of things-that-are-true. They're the type of fact you can verify by prodding or biting, but they go together with other types, equally certain, such as the fact that morning always comes. Or that the third little pig's house will never blow down in any telling of the story, no matter how hard the wolf huffs and puffs. Stories are *so*. Once you've established that they don't randomly alter, they have a role in the structure of reality. "The world is everything that is the case."

Not surprisingly, it doesn't matter much, at this stage when stories are satisfyingly invariant patterns, that they are fictions. The solidity of stories is also the quality that allows them to transport you; but to begin with they don't transport you very far. G. K. Chesterton pointed out that where a six-year-old is excited if someone opens a door in a story and finds a dragon on the other side, a two-year-old is excited enough if someone opens a door. The journeys that picture books take a small child on are very often journeys around the familiar. Burglar Bill in Janet and Allan Ahlberg's phenomenally successful picture book wears a stripy burglar's jersey and the traditional eye mask. The child who meets him has been introduced to a useful stock figure, maybe their first outlaw, and the wicked energy he represents is getting an outing. But what Burglar Bill does, once he has inadvertently stolen a baby, is to change nappies and warm up bottles, returning to the most familiar rituals with the difference that he is carrying a swag bag. The Ahlbergs' *Baby's Catalogue* takes this to its logical conclusion. It offers the pure pleasure of recognition, and nothing but. Its pages are arrays of feeder bottles and potties, little cardigans and high chairs, alternative mummies and daddies (recognizable as nicely observed types in the human zoo, so that even this virtually wordless book is already giving the adult intermediary who offers it to a child a little something for him- or herself, as the best picture books do, pleasing the social intelligence of adults on the quiet). In Shirley Hughes's *Alfie Gets in First,* Alfie, who is about three, excitedly slams the front door behind him, locking out his mum who's been wheeling his baby sister up the path. Through the letterbox she tries to talk him through the process of opening the door, helped by an ever-growing crowd of passersby.

Alfie's mum—to switch to judgments made by the adult eye— is a frizzy-haired anti-nuclear social worker from about 1985. Children don't do this stylistic/social disentangling, but they do make a global, intuitive decision about whether pictures represent the world as they know it to be. *Alfie Gets in First* will continue to speak directly to children about *their* front doors so long as Alfie's mum still looks reasonably contemporary. The

Shirley Hughes I had when I was two in 1966, *Lucy and Tom's Day,* doesn't do this anymore. Time has carried away the possibility of recognizing the baker, the milkman, and the newspaper boy who deliver things to Tom and Lucy's house. Daddy goes to work in a hat, Mummy stays at home in a print dress. But what I remember is how vivid the illustrations were, then as now led by the ink lines of Shirley Hughes's particular, rounded sense of children's faces. The ordinary scenes of Lucy and Tom's day affected me almost viscerally. The little red and blue train Tom played with seemed to be essence of toy; the tents they made of the dark red blankets in their nursery involved me in all the sensations that go with containment and hiding; the smeech of treacle on Tom's face at teatime had in it in concentrated form the comedy of disorder, the hilarity of things being out of place. *Lucy and Tom's Day* didn't bring in a single element I couldn't recognize from my own life. Its ordinary vision was quite intense enough.

But soon afterward the child's mind is being stocked, at speed, with all the figures and locales of story that have no equivalent whatsoever in their own lives. The other kind of story that small children are told—are equipped with, almost—before they can read, is the fairy tale. It can arrive as another, perhaps very beautiful, picture book, *Briar Rose* or *The Dancing Princesses* illustrated by Errol Le Cain; or in the form of a Disney video; but fairy stories come closer than most fictions to pure sequences of events, and no telling is definitive, though some are more orthodox than others. The tale is a running order, that's all. It can be stripped back to a flowchart like a software algorithm, and has been by the analysts who follow the Russian folklore formalist Vladimir Propp. It doesn't need pictures, it doesn't need to exist as a written-down text. You don't remember the *words* of a fairy story except for a very few ritualized formulas whose utterance is itself an event in the story and therefore belongs in its minimal flowchart. "Once upon a time." "Mirror, mirror, on the wall." To be said with three heavy emphases: "And she danced until she *dropped down dead!*" All a fairy tale needs, on the teller's side, is a speaking voice. Even a sense of occasion, with deliberate creation of atmosphere, isn't obligatory. Fairy tales survive perfectly well in the absence of firesides. They succeed partly because they can be reeled off pat by a busy adult to entertain a child while cooking or vacuuming a floor. Enough atmosphere is already there. The story's flowchart already builds in a demarcation from ordinary speech. "Once upon a time" is a marker to the effect that the language that follows isn't going to work the levers of immediate activity. Switch off your attention to cause and effect—to your surroundings—it says, and listen to this, sweetheart. . . . "Happily ever after" says that normal service will now be resumed.

In fairy tales, famously, character is destiny. Who the personages are, and what happens to them, are completely inseparable. You can predict what will happen to a good princess, just from the fact that she is a good princess. Her identity in the story maps out her future. Conversely, her goodness has no other aspects except those that are revealed by her marrying a handsome prince. That's all her goodness really means; though we will of course have seen it in action in acts of kindness or victimhood at the beginning of the story, so that we know it is there. In true fairy tales, as opposed to literary hybrids smuggling in the techniques of the novel, there are no individual characters, only types. Good princess; bad princess. Witches. Fairy godmothers. Genies. Kings who set tasks for suitors. These beings do not exist in the environment of the child who, at the same time as hearing about Snow White, is also thrilled by stories of door-opening. But the vocabulary of types is actually easier to acquire, in some ways, than knowledge about the child's own world, because the fairy-tale world is so perfectly self-explanatory. Every appearance by a witch is a complete, sufficient demonstration of what a witch *is*. In life, knowledge of other people's natures is both important and relatively hard to come by; it depends on a long loop of inferences moving gradually from the things people do and say to conclusions about what they're like. Children can afford to be much less cautious about the information in stories—much quicker to decide. Arthur Applebee asked a group of preschool children to tell him the characters of a list of animals. They were more certain of the stereotypical personalities of animals they could only have met in stories, such as brave lions or sly foxes, than of the characters of dogs or cats, where experience of specific dogs and cats came in to complicate the picture. Story characteristics are prepared for reception, so to speak; they're consistent, they don't contradict themselves, and they're dispensed at the pace that understanding demands.

To enjoy a story (including a fairy story) a child has to be curious about people. Also, they need to have reached the stage of socialization at which they understand emotional cause-and-effect between two or more actors on a story's stage. One person is angry, and the other person is sorry. Stories work once you know why. Autistic children, who never securely master interaction between people, never cotton on to narrative either. But once a child understands how different people's actions fit together to make up events, the information in stories flows with a purposeful density quite unlike the knowledge acquired one mosaic piece, or cloud droplet, or Seurat dot at a time, by participation in a world of behaving humans on whom the files are always open. Here's the first hint of the possibility that fiction can be an alternative to experience, rather than a representation of it.

Remote from our immediate experience fairy stories may be, but they can't be remote from our fears and desires, or we would find no urgency in them. "Only those voices from without are effective," wrote the critic Kenneth Burke in 1950, "which speak in the language of a voice within." Studies in the 1960s and 1970s of the stories children themselves tell at two and three found a relationship between how "socially acceptable" the actions in them were, and how much they took place in the recognizable, everyday world of the child's own experience. If they included taboo behavior like hitting a parent or wetting yourself, or major reversals of emotional security, like having a parent die or being abandoned by parents, they were less likely to have a realistic setting (69 percent versus 94 percent), less likely to feature the teller as a character (13 percent versus 39 percent), and much less likely to be told in the present tense (19 percent versus 56 percent). Dangerous things were moved further away in place and in time, and were not allowed to happen even to a proxy with the same name as the child. Children a year or two older no longer varied the present tense and past tense, because they consistently told all stories in the past tense; but they used settings in the same way, moving the troubling material outward into fantasy, into the zones where a story event reflected a real event less directly. To castles, pirate ships, space; to the forest. There the terrible things you might do, and the terrible things that might happen to you—not always easy to separate—can be explored without them jostling the images you most want to guard, the precious representations of your essential security. In fairy tales, after all, it is well known that people get their heads chopped off, or are eaten by wolves, or have to weave shirts of stinging nettles. A loose framework of retribution tends to balance up the books on cruelty in fairy stories, by the end; but bad things by no means happen only to bad people. Random acts of senseless violence come with the territory. They are natural there, you might say, along with skin-melting magical transformations, and blatant comic fusions involving noses and sausages, and the sudden sweeping arrival of great happiness.

And in a sense, this is necessary terrain. Its existence guards the existence of the safer lands of the imagination. You can make the argument purely on the conceptual level. Forbidden actions must be explored, by the logic of forbidding itself. To integrate a rule against something into a child's mind, so that it becomes their own, part of their own values and perceptions— as nearly all adults are opposed to murder on their own account, individually—it has to be understood; and for a rule to be fully understood involves imagining what happens when you break it. Or a parallel argument is available out of the psychoanalytic tradition, as Bettelheim extended it to fairy stories. A person can only grow to full maturity if his or her ego is able to draw on and transform the dark but powerful energies of the id. You must come to terms with your unconscious, and at an age when it would be too disturbing to confront unconscious forces under their own names, the best way to begin is by dealing with them through the symbols of story.

Either way, this is the fairy tale as a "thought experiment." Its typecast kings, its identikit princesses, are representatives of elements in our inward dramas. They are devoid of individual characteristics so that they may be universal. They are wholly good, wholly beautiful, wholly cruel, because they embody the impulses of love, delight, rage in their primal, unalloyed forms. They stand for pieces of us. The identifications are strong, but not blatant. For example, the wicked stepmother in a fairy tale, argued Bettelheim, embodies all the child's fears of being rejected by their real mother, and gives play to all the child's negative feelings about her, without disfiguring her necessarily loving image in the child's mind. The good mother has conveniently died, ceding her space in the tale to the hateable monsters who degrade Cinderella, and drive Snow White and Hansel and Gretel out into the forest. There is never a wicked natural mother in a fairy tale.

The fairy-tale cast may be limited, but Bettelheim's readings assigned the symbolic roles of the characters in different ways in the different groups of stories. In the stories where the third child—son or daughter—wins through his or her trials with the help of animals, the interpretation is fairly simple. The child, of course, is the ego; the raven released from the trap who in return fetches the diamond from the inaccessible mountain is a representative of the dark, instinctual id, just asking to be integrated into the personality; and the message is, do right by your unconscious, and your unconscious will do right by you. On the other hand, there are brother-and-sister stories where, with two of the psyche's pilgrims to play with, there's room to illustrate the dangers of the encounter with the bestial id, by having one be transformed into a creature of the wild. The brother drinks from a forbidden spring and shape-shifts into a stag or a swan, potent yet mute animals, emblems of a desire that has got out of hand. The sister—invariably the sister, nominated by her gender to play the role of the love that humanizes desire—retrieves him by mighty sacrifices, brings him back to his human form. Finally, Bettelheim pointed out, there's also a batch of stories in which the ego-portraying youngest child is (frankly) a twit, a twerp, a simpleton, a schlemiel, and yet conquers all by his foolishness, protected by the structure of the story in the same way that, as Bismarck joked, God protects "children, drunkards, and the United States of America." This, said Bettelheim, was a story for those moments when the child looked at the difference between his or her own littleness and the tough, complicated adult world, and needed an elementary reassurance that somehow, someday, he or she'd win through to the "kingdom" that signifies successful maturity.

Bettelheim published *The Uses of Enchantment* in 1974. The criticisms followed immediately. He had assumed that fairy tales were exclusively devised for children, when many of them were folk literature told by adults to adults. He'd ignored the differences between the national traditions. He'd discounted the realistic aspects of fairy-tale incidents. (In premodern Europe, where disease and childbirth carried off many women before the age of forty, there were an awful lot of stepmothers.) He'd analyzed the details of stories as if they had a fixed, authoritative existence, when in fact each version of a story represented only one momentary state of a fluid, combinatorial sea of possibilities. He didn't distinguish between a peasant story and an elegant courtier's retelling of it. These were the usual naiveties that result when psychoanalysis takes its search for the psyche's permanent structures into the changing, particular, context-determined material of culture. Similar complaints had been made about Freud's original use of Greek myths. But there has also been gradually strengthening criticism from within the constituency Bettelheim helped to form, which agrees with him that stories handle the deep material of the psyche.

It centers on Bettelheim's comfortable, even complacent, sense that a fairy-tale plot is a wholly *internal* drama. If kings and queens, stepmothers and godmothers are all names for pieces of the one self hearing the story, then what happens between them is only the psyche's own flow of transactions, wonderful at times, disturbing or savage at times, but with no reference beyond the child's set of internal representations of mother, father, sister, brother. But it is not easy to believe that the events of a fairy story really offer no reflection of what happens between people, as well as within one person. The question that must be answered to determine all story's moral status is: to whom are these things happening? Bettelheim replies, in effect: to symbols. A symbol dances in the red-hot iron shoes till she falls down dead. There is, however, an order in which a symbol creates its meanings, as feminists and others have pointed out. A character in a story exists in particular before it exists in general. A wicked stepmother is a woman before she is a symbol of what a child might fear in motherhood. The story "Snow White" therefore says things about gender, and the encounters of daughter, stepmother, father, and lover, before it can become a picture of a psychological process. The ostensible incidents of a story are more than screens, or the concrete analogies a young mind needs to deal with ideas. They are the means by which meaning arises at all. Every story has to be taken literally before it is taken any other way. Bettelheim's determination to skip this stage in a story's functioning could produce grotesque results.

Take his reading of "Bluebeard." It's the most famously horrible story in the European folk canon, condensing in extreme form either women's fears of what marriage may do to them, or male hatred of women, or both. The items on the flowchart common to all versions of the story are these. A young woman marries a lord, powerful, mysterious, and mysteriously alone despite a sequence of previous weddings. He goes away, leaving her a key, or an egg. He tells her she may look in every room of his castle except one. Since a prohibition in a fairy tale has exactly the same effect as an order, she does enter the forbidden room, which contains the dismembered bodies of all his other wives. This room is the heart of horror, with its revelation of atrocity concealed within normality, its terrible lack of explanation. It is the central symbol of male violence in folklore; because it can also be seen as womblike, a "bloody chamber" in a different sense, it was audaciously adopted by Angela Carter as a symbol for a female subjectivity aware of the danger in desire. I've never read it without feeling implicated. In the story Bluebeard's wife, appalled, lets slip the precious egg or key, and blood marks it indelibly with her knowledge. Bluebeard returns. She escapes. Or she doesn't: pick your version. Angela Carter had her mother ride up on a horse and shoot Bluebeard straight between the eyes with a cavalry pistol. Astonishingly, the moral traditionally tacked on to the story was that *curiosity* is dangerous—as if Bluebeard's murderous rage were the wife's fault for looking inside the chamber. Can anyone really have believed that if she hadn't, they would have lived happily ever after, the plot flipping over into "Beauty and the Beast" despite the butchery in the basement? Even more astonishingly, Bruno Bettelheim, concentration-camp survivor, effectively concurred. Leaping past the issue of who did what to whom in the chamber, and taking it as a symbol of forbidden knowledge in a general, sexual sense, he interpreted "Bluebeard" as a story about a woman's infidelity and—twisting time strangely—her husband's anger over it. Bettelheim's moral: "Women, don't give in to your sexual curiosity; men, don't permit yourself to be carried away by your anger at being sexually betrayed."

The movement for the reform of fairy tales that began in the 1970s was partly a response to this kind of thing—to readings that cheerfully saw villains as sympathetic embodiments of inner drives (if they were male) and blamed the victims (if they were female). Bettelheim had assumed that the roles of men and women, children and parents in prefeminist America effectively corresponded with psychological truth. When the roles changed, the idea that the female players of Faery (queen, witch, godmother) embodied the eternally defined aspects of Mom seemed less probable. Likewise, when child abuse imprinted itself on public consciousness, it no longer seemed tenable to suppose that the dark forest represented a territory that was safely separated from reality in every child's experience. The attempts to correct these things sometimes had a naivete mirroring the complacency they opposed. The first collections of feminist fairy tales—now much parodied—simply substituted ideally assertive heroines in place of ideally submissive ones: instead of Sleeping Beauty, the Biker Princess. Elsewhere, an attempt developed to sign up the terrible things that happen to children in fairy tales as the treasury of wounds without which no constituency can make its claim in the world of identity politics. "There is hardly a tale in the Grimms' collection"—argued the Grimm scholar and fairy-tale activist Jack Zipes, in 1995—"that does not raise the issue of parental oppression." And yet, "we rarely talk about how the miller's daughter is forced by her father into a terrible situation of spinning straw into gold, or how Rapunzel is locked up by her foster mother and maltreated just as children are often locked up in closets and abused today." *Often*: as if you could scarcely open a cupboard door these days without a corpse-white little starveling falling out, blinking furiously in the unaccustomed daylight. This is a mere inversion of Bettelheim's model of the child as perfectly safe and perfectly loved in his (always "his") suburban dream home.

The deeper risk of these insistences on the pure virtue, or pure victimhood, of the person in the tale with whom the child would most identify was that they operated as a kind of exorcism, driving evil entirely away from the subject, and therefore allowing no scope at all for its exploration. If evil appeared at all, the only place left for it was as an inexplicable quality of a cruel Them, as a tireless, persecuting force aimed *at* the heroine. Forever munched by adult wolves, she never ever felt wolfish herself. With the best intentions, the reformers had reinvented the plot of de Sade's *Justine*. But though the attempts to make stories prescribe desirable outcomes were naive, the reformers were right to recognize that prescription, laying down the law, is an inevitable part of what fairy tales do, and are. Every description, in a fairy story, of how people behave toward each other, with justice or injustice, is faintly, complicatedly, an endorsement. The certainty of story that allows a child to add it—with delight—to the category of "things that are so" also lends to its content the slight implication that this is how things ought to be. We cannot be told "Once there was a prince" without also being told (on some level and in some part) that it was right that there was a prince. What knits together out of nothing, and yet is solid enough to declare that it is so, recommends itself to us, although we don't receive the recommendation straightforwardly. In this lies the power, and the danger, of stories.

Rage being an important part of the three-year-old and four-year-old human condition, picture books for the age group find ways of telling stories about it, if they want to be true to experience. David McKee's *Not Now, Bernard,* for example: poor

Bernard can't get his parents to notice the monster that's after him, and when the monster eats him up, leaving just a training shoe behind, it can't draw their attention either. Very much Bernard-shaped and Bernard-sized, though with horns and scales, it has to have his supper of fish fingers and go to bed in his bed. "'But I'm a monster!' said the monster. 'Not now, Bernard,' said his parents."

The granddaddy of this school was Maurice Sendak's great *Where the Wild Things Are,* one of the few picture books to make an entirely deliberate, and beautiful, use of the psychoanalytic story of anger. It's a book of few, rhythmically inevitable words; and it has great visual authority too. Sendak's drawing has the stylized line and cross-hatched high definition of the German illustrations he admired as a child, while the reds and yellows and greens are the slightly faded colors of a 1940s toy theater, so that the book takes you to a sensory world somewhere between reality and play. Sendak knows exactly where. His hero Max, rampaging in a wolf suit, an id rampant, "made mischief of one kind / and another," until his mother sends him to bed supperless. But: "That night in Max's room a forest grew / and grew / and grew, until the walls became the wide world all around." I remember the impulse of delight I felt, strengthening each time, at the repetitions of "grew." Max dances. The uprights of Max's bed turn into trees and vines, every bedroom object staying in its place yet fading into vegetation within its outlines. This is the private forest of fantasy and the unconscious, from which Max journeys (in "a private boat") to meet the Wild Things of his anger. Yet he is traveling *out* too, to an encounter that the walls of his family cannot contain, which gives a real solitude to the events of the story, and makes his success substantial when he tames the Wild Things—his ramping, snorting, monstrous wishes—"by the magic trick of gazing deep into their yellow eyes without blinking once." Because he learns to have the energy of "the wild rumpus" without being devoured, when he grows lonely he can return to his bedroom where (after all) his supper is waiting for him. "And it was still hot," ends the story. But it isn't the family's love that kept him safe among the Wild Things. That's Max's own achievement. Although one reason for the story's emotional truthfulness is that the egotism of a small child still plainly frames the author as well ("Couldn't take the competition," Sendak said when asked why he had no children himself), *Where the Wild Things Are* is more than a transaction between symbols. It's about behavior as well as psychology, and the final reassurance is hard won: not entirely straightforward.

When *Where the Wild Things Are* was first published in the 1960s, it was seen as potentially disturbing. Bettelheim briefly condemned it. I had it, my parents being good liberals, and it didn't frighten me at all. It didn't occur to me to fear the bed-posts bursting into leaf, or the terrible teeth the Wild Things gnash, or the terrible eyes they roll. I thought the end took away the risk from it all. Now I wish I had worried more.

One January day when I was four, the au pair from Denmark who was helping out my parents while my sister was in the hospital took me for a walk in the woods. She'd been reading me the chapter in *Winnie the Pooh* where Pooh and Piglet go round and round the spinney in the snow, trying to catch the Woozle. "Let's go and find Piglet," she said. The Keele woods were under snow as well, that day. The snow was deep and powdery on the paths, and the trees were smoothed, white masses bowed under the weight of winter, like melted candles. We passed through a zone of little fir trees near the bottom of the steps down into the woods, leaving behind a trail of big footprints and a trail of little ones. (It's not a coincidence that Pooh and Piglet walking together in Ernest Shepard's illustrations have exactly the relative sizes of an adult and child going hand in hand.) And there, perched on the hollow stump of an oak, was Piglet, wearing a small red scarf exactly as in the pictures. The soft toy versions of the Disney characters did not exist yet. She had sewn him herself from gray and white cotton ticking. It was wonderful.

Looking back, I see that moment almost as the first step in a seduction. As a ten-year-old, as a teenager, as an adult, I've always wanted life to be more storylike; I've always reached out for treats, setups, situations that can be coaxed by charm and by the right kind of suggestively narrative talk into yielding something like the deliberate richness of an invented scene. Friends and lovers have known me as someone willing to say aloud sentences they thought could exist only on the page, in the hope that real time could be arranged and embroidered. I'd like words to be magic; or magnetic, attracting the events they name. Perhaps I first saw the chance of that when we found Piglet in the snow.

But at four I was only a hearer of stories. It isn't until we're reading stories privately, on our own account, that story's full seducing power can be felt. For the voice that tells us a story aloud is always more than a carrier wave bringing us the meaning; it's a companion through the events of the story, ensuring that the feelings it stirs in us are held within the circle of attachment connecting the adult reading and the child listening. To hear a story is a social act. Social rules, social promises, social bonds sustain us during it. Which is a kind of defense, when defense has been needed in reading. Yeshiva students turning the dangerous pages of the kabala would do so in groups, around their rabbi, so that the authority of the rabbi entered into the reading, and each was protected from the intensity of a solitary encounter with wild knowledge.

It is when, instead, we read it stumblingly for ourselves, when there's no other voice to link us into the web of relationship, that we feel the full force of the story's challenge: *You are alone, in a dark wood. Now cope.*

CHAPTER THREE

The Island

■ ■ ■

I learned to read around my sixth birthday. I was making a dinosaur in school from crepe bandage and toilet rolls when I started to feel as if an invisible pump was inflating my head from the inside. My face became a cluster of bumps on a taut sphere, my feet receded and turned into dangling limpnesses too far away to control. The teacher carried me home on her shoulders. I gripped the dinosaur in one hand. It was still wet with green and purple poster paint. After that things turned delirious. I had mumps; and one by one my sister, my mother, and my father all caught it from me. The house stayed convalescent in feeling till the last of us was better. It was a long quiet time of curtains closed during the day, and wan slow-moving adults, and bedsheets that seemed as big as the world when you lay in them, each wrinkle a canyon. On my sixth birthday my class came up the road and sang "Happy Birthday to You" in the front garden. It was too nice. I hid behind the curtain in my dressing gown and would not show myself at the upstairs window. Perhaps, for the very first time in my life, I was impatient to be done with a human encounter and to get back to my book. When I caught the mumps, I couldn't read; when I went back to school again, I could. The first page of *The Hobbit* was a thicket of symbols, to be decoded one at a time and joined hesitantly together. Primary schools in Britain now sometimes send home a photocopy of a page of Russian or Arabic to remind parents of that initial state when writing was a wall of spiky unknowns, an excluding briar hedge. By the time I reached *The Hobbit*'s last page, though, writing had softened, and lost the outlines of the printed alphabet, and become a transparent liquid, first viscous and sluggish, like a jelly of meaning, then ever thinner and more mobile, flowing faster and faster, until it reached me at the speed of thinking and I could not entirely distinguish the suggestions it was making from my own thoughts. I had undergone the acceleration into the written word that you also experience as a change in the medium. In fact, writing had ceased to be a thing—an object in the world—and *become* a medium, a substance you look through.

I. N. *In.* A. *In a.* H, o, l, e. *In a hole.* I, n, t, h, e, g, r, o, u, n, d. *In a hole in the ground.* L-i-v-e-d-a-h-o-b-b-i-t. *In a hole in the ground lived a hobbit . . .* And then I never stopped again.

Perhaps what has happened when writing seems to liquefy like this is that its effect on us has approximated the way thoughts move through our minds before we have phrased them in words at all. Perhaps writing at these times feels as if it has returned us by elaborate means to our minds' least-elaborated mode of operation. Least elaborated means most mysterious. The part of thinking that's easy to handle is the part that works by analogy with speech. Thinking in words, speaking our thoughts internally, projects an auditorium inside our skulls. Dark or bright, a shadow theater or a stage scorched by klieg lights, here we try out voices, including the voice we have settled on as the familiar sound of our identity, although it may not be what other people hear when we speak aloud. But that is the topmost of the linguistic processes going on in the mind. Beneath the auditorium runs a continuous river of thought that not only is soundless but is not ordered so it *can* be spoken. For obvious reasons, describing it is difficult. If I dip experimentally into the wordless flow, and then try to recall the sensations of it, I have the impression of a state in which grammar is present—for when I think like this I am certainly construing lucid relationships between different kinds of meaning, and making sense of the world by distinguishing between (for a start) objects and actions—but though there are so to speak nounlike and verblike concentrations in the flow, I do not solidify them, I do not break them off into word-sized units. Are there pictures? Yes; but I am not watching a slide show, the images do not come in units either. Sometimes there's a visual turbulence—rapid, tumbling, propelled—that doesn't resolve into anything like the outlines of separate images. Sometimes one image, like a key, like a presiding motif, will hold steady while a whole train of wordless thoughts flows from its start to its finish. A mountain. A closed box. A rusty hinge.

This is the layer of the mind that Chomskyans believe is our fundamental organ of linguistic ability, generated by the physical structure of our bodies. The assignment of a nounlike quality to one portion of the undivided flow, and a verblike quality to another, is grammar in its primary form. Whatever language a human being speaks when he or she goes on to put thought into words, the same structures underlie its particular rules about how meaning is expressed. We all have the same native tongue, deep down where "tongue" can only be a metaphor. If it is true that we process the written word so it communicates with us in the mind's own language, it is not surprising that writing can be so powerful. But of course a book does not really address us on this level. It's just a long, long string of symbols. When we read fluently, we pass the symbols by our eye so quickly that—like the frames of a film going through the gate of a projector—we cease to be aware of them as separate, and by a kind of persistence of vision, they seem to flow and move. A book is not another mind in communion with our own. It's just a software emulation of one, running on the hardware of our brains.

To achieve the effect, someone reading a book in English has to perform an intricate procedure at high speed: an act of double translation. First, you turn the printed characters into sounds. The alphabet is a set of arbitrary signs standing for the sounds of the spoken language; though not on a straightfor-ward one-to-one basis. Groups of letters build up to represent a single unit of sound, or phoneme, and the sound they make is dictated by the combination. The animal that claws your leg as you watch TV is called a *cat,* not a *kuh-ah-tuh,* although as children we're encouraged to pretend that each letter has its own unvarying sonic identity, to give us some purchase on the first stage of the code we're learning to crack. Then the second stage. Spoken language is itself an arbitrary code in which the sounds that the human lips, larynx, and tongue can produce— the phonemes—stand for the grammatical units, or morphemes, into which meaning is divided; though not on a straightforward one-to-one basis. So you translate writing into speech, and speech into meaning. Graphemes into phonemes, and phonemes into morphemes.

The complexity of this arrangement allows simplicity at its front end. An alphabetic writing system is extraordinarily com-pact. It uses a very small number of symbols to express the whole range of possible meanings in a language. You can read English, or Arabic, or Russian, or Hindi by learning between twenty and thirty different squiggles, plus a few punctuation marks representing pauses of different length and intensity. In the traditional form of lead type, the entire roman alphabet—that is, the entire European technology of writing—will fit across the palm of one hand. Abcdefghijklmnopqrstuvwxyz. Converted into binary code in the computers that have taken over from metal type as our culture's prime means of word storage, the alphabet could be completely displayed as a row of 130 zeroes and ones, or 26 five-digit numbers. (Although in fact it is conventionally represented in the universal ASCII code as the first 26 of 256 eight-digit numbers, leaving the rest available for numerals, punctuation, mathematical symbols, accents, pound and dollar and yen and euro signs, and alphabetic exotica such as the Latin æ, the German ß, and the Nordic ø.) The small space required to store an alphabet in the world is paralleled by its small demand on human memory. As a dinky, discrete little system it lodges in your head among the knowledge of how to do things. Like whistling or riding a bicycle, it can be retrieved from memory without any effort at all. But the economy of the code comes at the price of some cognitive heavy lifting. There's evidence that dyslexia is a significantly greater problem for children in the alphabet-using cultures than it is in China and Japan, where a written language based on ideograms asks the reader for a single, rather than a double, translation. With ideograms, the character correlates directly with the meaning: graphemes go straight to morphemes. On the other hand, the difficulty that alphabets internalize is externalized in Japan and China in the shape of the vast array of 35,000 or more characters. A Chinese poet or jurist, no matter how learned, will from time to time come across a character he doesn't recognize. In a sense, they never finish learning to read. Sparing dementia, stroke, or major head injury, a literate alphabet-user will never come across any *b* or *z* they can't read.

So the reading flows. So the reading flowed, when I was six with the yellow hardback copy of *The Hobbit* in my hands; and the pictures came. I went to the door of the hobbit hole with Bilbo as he let in more, and more, and more dwarfs attracted by the sign Gandalf had scratched there in the glossy green paint. I jogged along with him on his pony out of the Shire, away from raspberry jam and crumpets, and toward dragons. In *The Lord of the Rings,* this journey would become a transit from a little, naive space of comfort and tended fields into a dangerous world that besieged it. This time, it was only the natural progression of a story outward from home. Bilbo's life in Bag End was like real life, or at any rate like a bachelor fantasy of it, in which fifty is only just grown up, and the highest felicities are a pipe and convivial male company. The farther away from Bag End Bilbo went, the more purely he inhabited the world of adventure, and even of epic, until it seemed entirely proper for the dwarfs—who'd reminded me faintly of Grumpy and Sneezy and Doc during the comic washing-up scene at the beginning—to speak in archaic, elevated diction: "It was rightly guessed that I could not forbear to redeem the Arkenstone, the treasure of my house," said Thorin. Bilbo went on sounding like himself, chatty, fussy, scared, resourceful, prosy: *ordinary.* "Dear me! Dear me! I am sure this is all very uncomfortable." He was my passport to the mountains, and the caverns, and the hollow halls that the dwarfs had sung about back at Bag End, in a kind of promise that the book kept. I was ordinary too; if Bilbo could be there, so could I. Tolkien made him more extravagantly cowardly than

I thought of myself as being. "Then he fell flat on the floor, and kept on calling out 'struck by lightning, struck by lightning!' over and over again; and that was all they could get out of him for a long time." Therefore I believed it when he was also much braver than I could ever have been, riddling with Gollum in the dark or flattering Smaug as the dragon lay on his hoard of "gems and jewels, and silver red-stained in the ruddy light." The angle from which Tolkien looked at Bilbo set a limit on how scary events in *The Hobbit* could be. Nothing too awful could happen to someone who scurried like Bilbo, even if the goblins did set fire to the tree he was hiding in, and sing about skin crackling, eyes glazing, fat melting, and bones blackening. Even if the way out of that trap was an eagle ride, with Bilbo hanging on to a dwarf's legs for dear life, and the burning tree a red twinkle in the great dark lands swinging beneath him.

With Bilbo, I saw the peaks of the Misty Mountains. Mirkwood surrounded me, the forest of fairy tales in particularly gnarled, glimmering, spider-infested form. When Bilbo climbed a tree in Mirkwood to spy out the land, I burst through the canopy of the forest after days in the green gloom, and found the sea of bright breeze-ruffled leaves where velvet-black butterflies played. Not—I find now, rereading *The Hobbit*—that Tolkien described any of these things in the detail I remember. His was a speedy, storyteller's art. It made a few precise suggestions, supplied a few nodal adjectives from which the webwork of an imagined world could grow in a child's mind, and didn't linger. I made the pictures. I was lucky that my first book put me in the hands of a writer with such a conscious and decided idea of what a reader's imagination needed. Tolkien had trained himself on the hard nuggetlike specifics of Anglo-Saxon and Viking poetry, with its names for things that were almost spells, and its metaphors that were almost riddles. At six I had no idea that the sea had once been the whale-path, or that Tolkien had any predecessors when he had Bilbo boast to Smaug that he was "the clue-finder, the web-cutter, the stinging fly." He made bread, blood, and diamonds, and the bees as big as thumbs at Beorn's house, seem as fresh and vividly discovered as if they had just been thought of, for the first time in the world. What I did know explicitly was that while Tolkien's words were authoritative, his occasional black-and-white drawings in the text counted only as hints I was free to accept or refuse. What Middle Earth looked like was my business. Illustrations—I decided— were limitations. I had not been able to picture Bilbo's face, but I was comfortable with that. It seemed that he existed in a story-space in which it was not necessary that the points of Tolkien's description of a hobbit (round stomach, bright clothes, hairy feet, clever fingers, good-natured expression) should coalesce into one definite image; and in that, Bilbo was like my parents and my sister, whose ultimately familiar faces I found wouldn't come either when I shut my eyes and tried to summon them in the brown and purple dark behind my eyelids. No: the natural destiny of a story was to be a rich, unresolved swirl in my visual cortex, and any illustrator who tried to pin it down was taking a liberty.

At the same time, I couldn't read quite a lot of the words in *The Hobbit.* I had accelerated into reading faster than my understanding had grown. If I press my memory for the sensation of reading the second half of the book, when I was flying through the story, I remember, simultaneous with the new liquid smoothness, a constant flicker of incomprehensibility. There were holes in the text corresponding to the parts I couldn't understand. Words like *prophesying, rekindled,* and *adornment* had never been spoken in my hearing. No one had ever told me aloud to *behold* something, and I didn't know that *vessels* could be cups and bowls as well as ships. I could say these words over, and shape my mouth around their big sounds. I could enjoy their heft in the sentences. They were obviously the special vocabulary that was apt for the slaying of dragons and the fighting of armies: words that conjured the sound of trumpets. But for all the meaning I obtained from them, they might as well not have been printed. When I speeded up, and up, and my reading became fluent, it was partly because I had learned how to ignore such words efficiently. I methodically left out chunks. I marked them to be sorted out later, by slower and more patient mental processes; I allowed each one to brace a blank space of greater or lesser size in its sentence; I grabbed the gist, which seemed to survive even in sentences that were mostly hole; and I sped on.

I could do this because written English is an extremely robust system. It does not offer the user a brittle binary choice between complete comprehension and complete incomprehension. It tolerates many faults, and still delivers some sense. The reasons why were spelled out in 1948, by Claude Shannon of the Bell Telephone Company, as an incidental consequence of his mathematical research into the capacity of phone networks. Shannon's *Mathematical Theory of Communication* has been fruitful for cryptography, the science of chaos, literary theory, and the design of the Internet. It can also be applied to a six-year-old reading *The Hobbit*. Functionally speaking, there is no difference between a phone call one-third obscured by static on the line, a manuscript one-third eaten by mice, and a printed page one-third of whose words you don't know. Ignorance is just a kind of noise; and Shannon was interested in measuring how much of a message could be disrupted by the noise that's inevitable on any channel of communication, before it became impossible to decipher it.

He showed that information, in certain respects, flows through a network like heat flowing in nature. Like the entropy of atoms dispersing into ever greater randomness, an information flow's entropy could be measured, that is, the relative freedom every passing bit of information had to be any one of the symbols in the set that was in use, whether they were digits, or Morse dots and dashes, or letters of the alphabet. Conversely, it was possible to calculate how much of any information flow was not free to vary, since it was enforced by the structure of the message being transmitted. Suppose that the symbol set in question is the alphabet, and the message is being sent in English. After every letter q the next letter must be u. After every letter t the next letter is more likely to be h than any other; and may never be x. I comes before e except after c. All of these rules are expressions of the "redundancy" in English, indications of the ways in which the structure of the written language makes it less than random, and so restricts the possibilities for each element.

Shannon used "redundant" as a technical term. He did not mean that these rules were not essential to the intricate, delicate ways by which we convey meaning in writing. But the more highly structured a message was, the more its individual elements were indeed redundant in the sense that they could be dispensed with, and the more the message could be compressed, or edited, or subjected to electrical storms and mice and ignorance, without losing its intelligibility. If u invariably followed q, then u really added no extra information to q. U could therefore be taken away and nothing would be lost from the meaning.

The person receiving the message—Shannon concluded—would be able to understand it adequately if noise removed any amount of the message up to the maximum redundancy built into the message by its structure. He did a quick statistical survey of written English, and calculated that it had a redundancy of about 50 percent. Up to half of an English text could be deleted before doing such critical damage to its message that you'd give up and say Eh? A page of *The Hobbit* could have had Liquid Paper rained down on up to half its words, or been cloven by dwarfish axes so long as it was not quite cloven in twain, and I would have been able to follow it. My mental blanking when the print spelled out a-d-o-r-n-m-e-n-t could not stop the flow of story from the book into my mind.

I found that the gaps in the text where I did not know words began to fill themselves in from the edges, as if by magic. It was not magic. I was beginning to acquire the refined and specialized sense of probability that a reader gets from frequent encounters with the texture of prose: not just the probabilities of which letters and words would follow each other that Shannon had studied, in his brief survey of language as one transmission system among many, but all the larger probabilities governing the shapes of paragraphs and chapters, all the way up to the overarching rules—or meta-rules—of story itself, that grand repertoire of beginnings and middles and ends. Unknown words picked up meaning from the words around them, meanings that worked well enough in context, though sometimes I was completely wrong.

I remember there was an intermediate stage when strange words did not yet quite have a definite meaning of their own, but possessed a kind of atmosphere of meaning, which was a compromise between the meanings of all the other words that seemed to come up in conjunction with the unknown one, and which I had decided had a bearing on it. The holes in the text grew over, like this. The empty spaces thickened, took on qualities that at first were not their own, then became known in their own right. But it was not a process like scabs growing over cuts. That's too thick, too brown, too fibrous, too *organic* a metaphor. Writing might flow like thought, but it was still a constructed thing. That was part of its appeal to me, that it retained an intricate, *made* separateness from bodies, mumps, and families. Imagine instead a vast dome built up from countless panels of stained glass. Some panels are missing. As you gaze at an empty segment of the dome, the space shimmers, and into it are infused, like vibrations in the air, both the fire-opal blue from the panel to the right, and the lemony gold from the panel to the left. They harden, and now there is glass there, of a color somewhere between the two: a citric green perhaps.

Now that I hardly ever spell out a word I do not know, and the things that puzzle me in books do not lie in individual words but in the author's assumption of shared knowledge about the human heart (never my strong point), I still have, like everybody, words in my vocabulary that are relics of that time. The words we learned exclusively from having books infill their meaning for us are the ones we pronounce differently from everyone else. Or, if we force ourselves to say them the public way, secretly we believe the proper pronunciation is our own, deduced from the page and not corrected by hearing the word aloud until it was too late to alter its sound. The classic is "misled," said not as *mis-led* but as *myzled*—the past tense of a verb, "to misle," which somehow never comes up in the present tense. In fact, *misled* never misled me. One of mine is "grimace." You probably think it's pronounced *grimuss,* but I know different.

It's *grim-ace* to rhyme with "face." I'm sorry, but on this point, the entire English-speaking human race except me is wrong.

For me, such words demonstrated the autonomy of stories. In stories, words you never heard spoken nonetheless existed. They had another *kind* of existence. They acted—upon objects likewise made of words. Goblins burrowed in the earth, elves sang songs in the trees: those were the obvious wonders of reading, but behind them lay the fundamental marvel that, in stories, words could command things to be. They commanded events to happen, each one generating its subtle, supple tone, and therefore they commanded feeling, which was not true of the ordinary world, where protestations did not abolish unease, however vehemently they were made, and where I always feared that however strongly I pledged my allegiance to the family, some terrible countertruth of rage and rejection was pooled inside me, in the sump of my psyche. In stories, if an author said it, it was so. Maybe it is true, as I argued in the previous chapter, that all sentences tell a story of sorts; but the sentences *in* a story have a special power. In a world wholly composed of words, words hit no obstructions, have no limit on their effectiveness. They can take you elsewhere.

The home of the massed possibilities of story was the public library. Keele University ran a free bus service for the cleaners who came up from the towns of the Potteries to Keele Park to wax the floors of the university departments and clean the students' rooms. Anyone could use it, and from when I was about seven or so, I regularly rode the bus down the hill on my own to visit the library in Newcastle-under-Lyme. The bus turned out of the park gates, and suddenly, instead of being inside the small horizon of the campus, cupped on the hilltop round its lakes and woods, the view opened onto a long valley full of housing estates and pit winding gear and factories. In the fields sloping down to the town, bullocks nosed at blackberry bushes on rainy mornings. Rooks cawed in the trees. At night the valley twinkled with sodium lights. Beyond the new roundabout at the foot of Keele Bank, the weirdly center-less conurbation of the Potteries began, as large as a city altogether, but never as concentrated. There were five small-town provincial High Streets, five sets of Victorian civic architecture. Newcastle's core was red sandstone, scorched by nineteenth-century industrial soot.

As I first remember it, it still had a cattle market, and one of those courtly antique grocery emporiums smelling of cheese and coffee beans, where the money my parents paid over for food in neat waxed-paper packages vanished into the ceiling up pneumatic tubes, and the change came jingling down other tubes into round brass dishes the size of an ashtray. But both those holdouts from the past had vanished by the time I was taking myself to the library, and judged by the slow time of seven-year-olds, when several epochs will fit into one year, they were already a long time ago. Now was now, the modern, the proper, the natural year 1972. 1969 was ancient history, 1975 was science fiction. (I saw "1975" printed in my guide to the Ffestiniog Railway—it was the year they were going to finish a station—and I just stared at it, amazed that this moment that did not exist yet could be fitted into an ordinary sentence as if it were something solid and dependable.) The shops along the Ironmarket had posters of Slade, T-Rex, and the Osmonds for sale. When I bought a packet of Sweet Cigarettes for four new decimal pence (10¢) there was a cigarette card of the space race inside. Down Bridge Street there was an Indian restaurant where I had been with my dad and adventurously eaten a biriani. When my Coke came, there'd been a slice of lemon floating in it. Amazing sophistication!

The town seemed just as glamorous to me as the parkland up the hill, only with a different orientation, a different job to do in my imagination. For a long time, just as I set any wild scene in Keele woods, whenever I read a story set somewhere urban, I borrowed Newcastle in my mind's eye as the setting. Newcastle figured as London, as Paris; tweaked with columns, it was Rome, with a few pointy bits on the roofs it was Chinese. Later, when I read *To Kill a Mockingbird,* I made it into the Deep South. "Maycomb was an old town," wrote Harper Lee, "but it was a tired old town when I knew it." I upped the temperature, and let the rooflines sag. I put Maycomb town jail in the arcade by the town hall where they sold the éclairs. Scout and Jem Finch lived where Woolworth's stood, and Boo Radley's house was the hairdresser's a few doors along, with a veranda slapped on the front and yellow grass set growing between the paving stones.

The library was a brand-new concrete and glass block at the end of the Ironmarket, just before the civic gardens by the roundabout where the rose trees were trimmed into skinny public bouquets. In the window, leaflets about passing your driving test were stapled to a corkboard, and there was a poster, put up well in advance, encouraging you to PLANT A TREE IN SEVENTY-THREE. To get to the children's section, you turned sharp left inside and down the stairs into a long basement room lit by the blue-white of fluorescent tubes. The issue desk was at the far end, next to the floor-level picture books and colored stools for the tinies; two or three wire twirlers of paperbacks tried to tempt you on your way out, like the chocolates for impulse purchasers at supermarket checkouts, but at that time library budgets ran to hardbacks as a matter of course, and, anyway,

paperbacks were for owning yourself. The library's true treasure was the A–Z Children's Hardback Fiction, running the
whole length of the right-hand wall on metal shelves arranged
in big U-shaped bays. Every book had its dust wrapper sealed
onto the cover in heavy-duty plastic, soup-proof, thumb-proof,
spaghetti-hoop-proof. Every book bore a yellow Dewey Decimal
code number on a sticker on the spine. I approached them
slowly, not with reverence exactly, but with the feeling that the
riches in the room needed to be handled with some kind of
grateful attention to their ordered abundance. Also, I knew that
once I'd chosen my four books, the multiple possibilities of the
library would shrink down to that finite handful. I hated to be
hurried out of the great, free bazaar.

Library visits have been a ritual in well-regulated childhoods in Britain and America for seventy years now. I recognize
my own history in Randall Jarrell's 1944 vision of worlds smol-
dering under the stone roof of the Carnegie Library in Pittsburgh, and the books opening out upon a

> . . . country the child thought life
> And wished for and crept to out of his own life.

Or in Ray Bradbury's raptured evocation of the contrast
between the tame apparatus of the library on the one hand—
with its benevolent ladies presiding and the quintessence of
order in the metallic *ker-chunk* of the date stamper—and the
wilds it contained. This is *Something Wicked This Way Comes*:

> The library deeps lay waiting for them.
> Out in the world, not much happened. But here in the
> special night, a land bricked with paper and leather, any-
> thing might happen, always did. Listen! and you heard

ten thousand people screaming so high only dogs feathered their ears. A million folk ran toting cannons, sharpening guillotines; Chinese, four abreast, marched on forever. Invisible, silent, yes, but Jim and Will had the gift of ears and noses as well as the gift of tongues. This was a factory of spices from far countries. Here alien deserts slumbered. Up front was the desk where the nice old lady, Miss Watriss, purple-stamped your books, but down off away were Tibet and Antarctica, the Congo . . .

But Bradbury writes as if the stories burst out of their library bindings on their own. I never found that. For me, they had to be stalked, sampled, weighed, measured, sniffed, tasted, often rejected. There were so many possibilities that the different invitations each book made would have blended together, if they had been audible, into a constant muttering hum. To hear the separate call of a book, you had to take it up and detach it from all the other possibilities by concentrating on it, and giving it a little silence in which to work. Then you learned what it was offering. Be a Roman soldier, said a book by Rosemary Sutcliffe. Be an urchin in Georgian London, said a Leon Garfield. Be Milo, "who was bored, not just some of the time but all of the time," and drives past the purple tollbooth to the Lands Beyond. Be where you can hear cats talking by tasting the red liquid in the big bottle in a chemist's shop window. Be where magic works easily. Be where magic works frighteningly. Be where you can work magic, but have to conceal being invisible or being able to fly from the eyes of the grown-ups. Be an Egyptian child beside the Nile, be a rabbit on Watership Down, be a foundling so lonely in a medieval castle that the physical ache of it reaches to you out of the book; be one of a gang of London kids playing on a bombsite among the willowherb and the loosestrife, only fifteen years or so before 1972 but already far, far into the past. Be a king. Be a slave. Be Biggles. All this was there in the library basement, if you picked up the books and coaxed them into activity, and uncountably much more besides. There can have been only five or six bays along the right-hand wall, but they seemed inexhaustible.

Books could vary more than virtually anything else that went around in the world under one name. They infused me with incompatible, incomparable emotions. Arthur Ransome's *Swallows and Amazons* series, for example, apart from giving me an enormous crush on Captain Nancy Blackett of the Amazons, always reminded me of my cousins, a large practical family in Cambridgeshire who messed about in canoes on fen rivers just (I thought) like the Ransome children did in sailing boats on Lake Windermere. Idylls of meticulous detail, instructive about semaphore and surveying and gold refining, the twelve Ransome books let me try out a counterlife for size: a wonderfully prosaic alternative to my own small, dreamy, medically unlucky family of four. Here, brothers and sisters were robust. They milled around. The parents waved the adventurers off at the dock on page one, and no intense spotlight of anxiety fell on anyone. The stories blended with the life I imagined my cousins had. Without having to feel disloyal, I could experiment, reading Arthur Ransome, with the idea of belonging to that other version of family life that existed over at my aunt and uncle's house, with its dinghy in the garage, and its big Pyrex pots of stew and mounds of boiled potatoes at mealtime instead of our Elizabeth David–inspired experiments with risotto and pasta.

On the other hand, Ian Serraillier's *The Silver Sword* sent me recoiling back into family safety and family certainty. I wanted to believe that Jan the orphan in *The Silver Sword,* who leads a feral existence in the ruins of wartime Warsaw, was much older than me, so I couldn't possibly be expected yet to face the dangerous world alone. I'd had a vision of life with nothing to depend on, when I was changing trains in London on my own, carefully equipped with a page of instructions in my father's clearest handwriting. As I rode the escalator up from the Underground into the big, gusty dark of a rail terminus, gripping the sheet of paper, I thought suddenly: what if I had no instructions to get me home? What if I had no home to get to? What if my life, right now, got lost in these wild spaces full of strangers and never emerged again? And these were only two points on the spectrum of moods represented in Children's Fiction A–Z. When I made my choice, and walked back up the Ironmarket from the library to the bus stop, I knew I might have melancholy tucked under my arm; or laughter; or fear; or enchantment.

Or longing. My favorite books were the ones that took books' implicit status as other worlds, and acted on it literally, making the window of writing a window into imaginary countries. I didn't just want to see in books what I saw anyway in the world around me, even if it was perceived and understood and articulated from angles I could never have achieved; I wanted to see things I never saw in life. More than I wanted books to do anything else, I wanted them to take me *away.* I wanted exodus. I was not alone. Tolkien believed that providing an alternative to reality was one of the primary properties of language. From the moment humans had invented the adjective, he wrote in *On Fairy Tales,* they had gained a creator-like power to build elsewheres.

The mind that thought of *light, heavy, grey, yellow, still, swift,* also conceived of magic that would make heavy things light and able to fly, turn grey lead into yellow gold, and the still rock into swift water. If it could do the one, it could do the other; it inevitably did both. When we can take green from grass, blue from heaven, and red from blood, we have already an enchanter's power—upon one plane; and the desire to wield that power in the world external to our minds awakes.

Anyone, he said, could use "the fantastic device of human language" to mint a new coin for the imagination, such as *the green sun.* The green sun had no value, though, unless it was given a sky to rise in where it would have the same natural authority as the real yellow sun in the real sky. And after the sky, you had to invent the earth; and after the earth, the trees with their times of flowering and fruiting, and the inhabitants, and their habits of thought, and their manners of speech, their customs and clothing, down to the smallest details that labor and thought could contrive. To sustain a world inside which the green sun was credible required "a kind of elvish craft," "story-making in its primary and most potent mode." In fact Tolkien wanted to believe that fantasy was the highest form of art, more demanding than the mere reflection of men and women as they already were. He wanted to be able to look outward to story, and have it contain all that you might look inward to find, then more besides.

But I knew there was a fundamental division between stories set entirely in another world, and stories that traveled out to another world from the everyday reality of this one. Some books I loved were in the first category. Tolkien himself, of course: the year I was eight, I read *The Lord of the Rings* for the first time. I skipped through Pippin and Merry's adventures in Gondor in the middle to get back to Sam and Frodo and the

Ring. I identified their journey as *the* story. Mordor formed in my mind, the blasted land, the cratered land, roofed in rolling smoke from Mount Doom, and lit by gouts of flame like the North Sea oil-rig flares I'd seen on television. The orcs were leathery, mutant, nightmare grunts, marching to and fro on the military roads. Frodo and Sam crept between, hobbit knight and hobbit squire, the drama of their desperation shrunk to a speck by the hellish grandeur of the surroundings, their only hope to be so small the all-powerful enemy did not notice them, and all the while Gollum trailed inexorably after on squelching feet. For some reason, I pictured Gollum as a small upright green croco-dile, with the pale lantern eyes Tolkien specified. I read the book in three transported, mesmerized days. On the paper jacket of my father's old hardback edition, the Eye of Sauron was drawn in red. It seemed to stare at me. Whenever I was called for a reluc-tant meal break, I took care to leave the book facedown.

Later, I discovered and cherished Ursula Le Guin's *Earthsea* novels. They were utterly different in feeling, with their archi-pelago of bright islands like ideal Hebrides, and their guardian wizards balancing light and dark like yin and yang. All they shared with Tolkien was the deep consistency that allows an imagined world to unfold from its premises solidly, step by cer-tain step, like something that might really exist. Consistency is to an imaginary world as the laws of physics are to ours. The spell-less magic of Earthsea gave power to those who knew the true names of things: a beautifully simple idea. Once I had seen from the first few pages of the first book, *A Wizard of Earthsea,* that Le Guin was always going to obey her own rules, I could trust the entire fabric of her world. Though I resisted its les-sons. The student wizard Ged cracks open the surface of the night and releases a shadow version of himself into the world, a

Jungian clot of personal darkness, that hunts him till he turns to face it and incorporates it back into himself where it belongs, by naming it with its true name: his own. I resolutely thought of the shadow as a bogey alien to Ged, and wondered why he wasn't different at the end of the book when that dark thing was inside him. You cannot outrun yourself, the story said: a deeply unwelcome thought to me. I didn't go to the worlds of story to be reminded that on a dark road your anger and your cruelty pace just behind you, daring you to turn your head, unless you let them travel safely within you.

The books I loved best were in the second category—the ones that started in this world and took you to another. Earthsea and Middle Earth were separate. You traveled in them in imagination as you read Le Guin and Tolkien, but they had no location in relation to this world. Their richness did not call to you at home in any way. It did not lie just beyond a threshold in this world that you might find if you were particularly lucky, or particularly blessed. I wanted there to be the chance to pass through a portal, and by doing so to pass from rusty reality with its scaffolding of facts and events into the freedom of story. I wanted there to be doors. If, in a story, you found the one panel in the fabric of the workaday world that was hinged, and it opened, and it turned out that behind the walls of the world flashed the gold and peacock blue of something else, and you were able to pass through, that would be a moment in which all the decisions that had been taken in this world, and all the choices that had been made, and all the facts that had been settled, would be up for grabs again: all possibilities would be renewed, for who knew what lay on the other side?

And once opened, the door would never entirely shut behind you either. A kind of mixture would begin. A tincture of this world's reality would enter the other world, as the ordinary children in the story—my representatives, my ambassadors—wore their shorts and sweaters amid cloth of gold, and said *Crumbs!* and *Come off it!* among people speaking the high language of fantasy; while this world would be subtly altered too, changed in status by the knowledge that it had an outside. E. Nesbit invented the mixing of the worlds in *The Amulet,* which I preferred, along with the rest of her magical series, to the purely realistic comedy of the Bastables' adventures in *The Treasure Seekers* and its sequels. On a gray day in London, Robert and Anthea and Jane and Hugh travel to blue sky through the arch of the charm. The latest master of worlds is Philip Pullman. Lyra Belacqua and her daemon walk through the aurora borealis in *Northern Lights*; in the next book of the *Dark Materials* trilogy, *The Subtle Knife,* a window in the air floats by a bypass in the Oxford suburbs; in *The Amber Spyglass,* the last installment, access to the eternal sadness of the land of the dead is through a clapped-out, rubbish-strewn port town on the edge of a dark lake.

As I read I passed to other worlds through every kind of door, and every kind of halfway space that could work metaphorically as a threshold too: the curtain of smoke hanging over burning stubble in an August cornfield, an abandoned church in a Manchester slum. After a while, I developed a taste for the transitions so subtle that the characters could not say at what instant the shift had happened. In Diana Wynne Jones's *Eight Days of Luke,* the white Rolls-Royce belonging to "Mr. Wedding"—Woden—takes the eleven-year-old David to Valhalla for lunch, over a beautiful but very ordinary-seeming Rainbow Bridge that seems to be connected to the West Midlands road system. I liked the idea that the borders between the worlds could be vested in modern stuff: that the green and white signs on motorways counting down the miles to London could suddenly show the distance to Gramarye or Logres. But my deepest loyalty was unwavering. The books I loved best of all took me away through a wardrobe, and a shallow pool in the grass of a sleepy orchard, and a picture in a frame, and a door in a garden wall on a rainy day at boarding school, and always to Narnia. Other imaginary countries interested me, beguiled me, made rich suggestions to me. Narnia made me feel like I'd taken hold of a live wire. The book in my hand sent jolts and shimmers through my nerves. It affected me bodily. In Narnia, C. S. Lewis invented objects for my longing, gave forms to my longing, that I would never have thought of, and yet they seemed exactly right: he had anticipated what would delight me with an almost unearthly intimacy. Immediately I discovered them, they became the inevitable expressions of my longing. So from the moment I first encountered *The Lion, the Witch and the Wardrobe* to when I was eleven or twelve, the seven Chronicles of Narnia represented essence-of-book to me. They were the Platonic Book of which other books were more or less imperfect shadows. For four or five years, I essentially read other books because I could not always be rereading the Narnia books. I had a book-a-day habit to support, and there were only seven of them after all. But in other books, I was always seeking for partial or diluted reminders of Narnia, always hoping for a gleam of the sensation of Narnia. Once felt, never forgotten.

"Let us . . . suppose a violation of frontier," wrote C. S. Lewis, defending fantasy in 1949, the year he completed *The Lion, the Witch and the Wardrobe*. It was his first attempt to write for children. But though the form was new to him, by then he had

been devoted for many years to the idea that it might be possible
to cross the frontier of ordinary life.

It was philosophy that taught him the nature of the frontier,
and at first he had not believed there were doors. As an atheist
student in Oxford after the First World War, he subscribed to
the school of critical thought that had begun in the Enlightenment in the work of Hume and Kant. Traditionally, philosophy
had tried to answer ultimate questions about freedom and
truth, the nature of humanity and the nature of God. This, on
the other hand, was a program of stripping away the curlicues
of metaphysics that previous philosophy's search for answers
had woven around human experience. Critical philosophy's bite
had recently been renewed in Oxford, and it was in the process
of modulating into the logical positivism of Bertrand Russell
and the young Wittgenstein. From one critical philosopher to
another, emphasis and interpretation varied, but the map of the
universe that they drew remained beautifully bare and plain.
We have to see through philosophical eyes here. Although
human life as directly experienced is at the center of the map, it
is thought of in the abstract, without any of the particular coloring we learn from our curiosity about individual lives and
their differences. So forget anecdotes and incidents. Let logic
take the place of biography. Make your mind into a sheet of
white paper.

Now imagine a circle. Inside the circle is the territory of
sense-experience: everything we ever touch, see, taste, hear, or
smell, and know to be the case because we sense it. This includes
not just the initial sensations but all the factual knowledge that
develops from them, all the feelings and deductions that pertain
to our existence as bodies in the world: everything. Outside the
circle lies the domain of metaphysics, defined as the class of all

concepts whose existence cannot be demonstrated logically from the data of our senses. Here be, not dragons, but such postulates as God, eternity, perfection, a meaning to events that we do not put there ourselves, ultimate purpose for human actions. Whether or not the ideas outside the circle are nonsense according to the ordinary understanding of the word—the philosophers disagreed—they are certainly non-sense judged by the criteria used inside the circle. Kant thought the object of philosophy was to remind us not to use the intellectual methods molded by factual experience on the nebulous stuff beyond experience. We should not think about God as if God were a person in the world; we should not think about heaven as if it were another place of the sort we are already familiar with. The only function that Kant could see in philosophy for the space beyond the circle was that it might supply us with imaginary reference points toward which we could gaze. Like a fixed star, the idea of perfection, for example, might be useful to navigate by even if it could never be reached. Otherwise, it was a vacuum out there. Wittgenstein went further in the *Tractatus Logico-Philosophicus*, published in 1921. For him, language ended at the boundary of the circle, and with it, existence in any sense that language was capable of describing. It was not even meaningful to talk about going "beyond" the boundary. There was no outside. The line of the frontier was the curved edge of the universe. It had no other side. You could only talk about human existence happening against a background of profound mystery.

C. S. Lewis signed up to this map, but he did not like it. His imagination contradicted it; needed to contradict it, perhaps. Lewis the abrasive dialectician who, it was reported, "seems to think that Plato is always wrong," had been a teenage officer on the Western Front. Before that, he was a confident, absorbed child in Ulster, feeling no need for friends outside his family, impatiently instructing his big brother where to stand and what to be in their games. Suddenly, when he was nine, his mother died of cancer. His father, driven to distraction by grief, turned to his sons for emotional support; they shrank back, unable to bear what felt like an invitation to abandon all their defenses. Since then, it had not seemed fundamentally safe to Lewis to look in the world for the sustenance that once, traumatically, had been snatched away when he was depending on it. After that, food for the heart seemed to him to come from over the hills and far away, from a source that receded, if you went looking for it, like the end of the rainbow.

He was a romantic. While he did respond to the intellectual zeal with which critical philosophy took a hank of wire wool to the ground-in grease of previous philosophical systems and began to scrub, the kind of beauty he looked for was very different from the stark sort implied by the bare circle on the map, when the world's outlines were reduced to the lines of geometry, without decoration, without thickening emotion. Wittgenstein designed a house in Vienna built in white concrete. He sat in a deck chair in an empty room, engaged in pure mentation. Lewis could not have abided this aesthetic starvation diet. He preferred (as he wrote later) "that unnameable something, desire for which pierces us like a rapier at the smell of a bonfire, the sound of wild ducks flying overhead, the title of *The Well at the World's End,* the opening lines of 'Kubla Khan,' the morning cobwebs in late summer . . ." In the same piece of writing—the preface to the 1943 edition of his allegory *The Pilgrim's Regress*—he analyzed that "intense longing," remembering how as a child he had felt it for distant hillsides, as an adolescent for an imaginary beloved or for the occult, as a scholar for intellectual mastery. "But every one of these impressions is wrong ... Every one of these sup-posed *objects* for the Desire is inadequate to it." When he pressed these things for the sensation that they had seemed to hold out to him, it slipped away. "It appeared to me therefore that if a man diligently followed this desire ... he must come out at last into the clear knowledge that the human soul is made to enjoy some object that is never fully given ... in our present mode of subjec-tive and spatio-temporal existence." If the map was right, though, there was no other mode of existence on offer. If the world ended in a one-sided wall, where was happiness to be found?

Then in 1929 Lewis was converted to Christianity. For him, as it had been for the early Christians who broke the rules of Roman society, it was a deeply transgressive religion, in the lit-eral sense of the word. It instructed you to trans-gress, that is, to "go across," a whole set of lines that divided radically different states of being. When pagan Romans looked at Christians, they saw people who ignored some of the boundaries essential to civ-ilized existence. Instead of segregating the dead in cemeteries beyond the city walls, for example, to keep the taint of mortality out of the world of the living, the Christians lived among the dead on shockingly intimate terms, by burying them in their churches, and founding whole shrines around the flesh or bones of particularly honored corpses. They were following the example of the Jesus who had deliberately broken the laws of the Sabbath; who had violated ritual purity by sitting down to eat with prostitutes and with the agents of his country's occu-pying power; who had, Christians believed, crossed from life into death and back into life again at his resurrection. As a Chris-tian, you responded to this great intervention by God in the life of this world, by coming out of your old sinful existence in a nature corrupted by sin, and crossing through the waters of baptism, into a new and redeemed life with God. You might look the same, but you had declared that ultimately you depended on the love of God to nourish and sustain you, rather than on the food-and-sex-and-shelter-providing fertility of nature. Your connection beyond the world took priority. In the end you would leave this bodily life altogether, and travel into eternity on the far side of death. You would go to the source of all promises, where the living water flowed, and (according to the Book of Revelation) "there shall be no more death, neither sorrow, nor crying, neither shall there be any more pain: for the former things are passed away."

Among the things this meant to Lewis, one was that the border around sense-experience was now permeable. He had found an infinitely large object for his longing, and the map was changed. Its topology was still the same. There was still a circle, and it still divided two domains, one inside, one outside. But the space beyond the circle, which had been bare and empty, which had signified the vacuum of metaphysics, now represented a fullness that could only be dreamed of, and yearned for, from within the boundary line. Beyond the circle, everything was richer, and more solid, and more *real*. "If we must have a mental picture to symbolize Spirit, we should represent it as something *heavier* than matter," he wrote. From being someone who thought that Plato was always wrong, with his view of this life as a mere play of shadows cast by true objects elsewhere, he had become someone who thought that Plato was almost always right. ("It's all in Plato, all in Plato: bless me, what *do* they teach them at these schools!" says Digory at the end of *The Last Battle,* the last of the Narnia stories.) If what we see in the distance here does not satisfy when we reach it, and take it into our hands, that's because it is only an insubstantial ghost of the real thing, which we will find, in time, beyond the line.

And this did not apply just to spiritual things, and to elusive sensations, but to the entire fabric of the physical world. A deeply carnal individual, Lewis always imagined heaven in carnal, you might say hypercarnal, terms. It was not just the place where we will encounter immortal love, and see the true stars shine by comparison with which the stars of our familiar sky are dim, sad glowworms. It was also the home of the immortal sausage, more brown, more popping, more savory in its skin than the shadow sausages we know now; of immortal beer, and immortal tobacco, and all the other things Lewis enjoyed. It was the place where feeling would reach its fruition, its consummation. There, when you did the Keatsian thing, and burst joy's grape against your palate fine, a hand grenade of true grapishness would go off in your mouth, and send its total message of cool pale green flesh, sweet and yet acidic, to overwhelm every nerve in your body.

Of course, such fierce delight would be too much for us in our present bodies. If we touched perfection now, it would hurt us. In *The Great Divorce*, Lewis imagined the sad shades in Hell being allowed to visit Heaven, and finding the grass underfoot as sharp as spikes of diamond—a speculation similar, really, to the old laddish gag that Superman and Lois Lane couldn't have sex because, when he ejaculated inside her, his supersonic super sperm would blow a hole in her. But fortunately, when we are raised by God in our shining new bodies of new flesh, we shall be as strong as everything else in the true kingdom, and capacity shall at last be exactly equal to desire. Desire was the right word, in all its connotations, the sexual ones included. Lewis took a completely orthodox but rather marginal point of Christian doctrine and made it central to his belief. It was axiomatic that no sinful act could bring the sinner any substantial reward. You might be tempted by the idea that the sin would bring you a full, overflowing, pleasure, but when you actually succumbed, you'd find out that all you got was a flat, empty sensation. The apples of Sodom taste of ashes. This happened because sins were parodies, or perversions, of the legitimate pleasures God had ordained for human beings. In that case, reasoned Lewis, if you resisted sins in this life, every pleasure they held out delusively to you now would be supplied in reality and in overwhelming abundance in the greater life to come. *Every* pleasure, though we might no longer recognize them as sexual once they had shed their mortal connections with biology.

Stars, sausages, diamonds. Lewis's map could not remain the diagram it had been for the philosophers. It ceased to be minimalist and monochrome. It burst out, like the page of the magician's book in *The Voyage of the Dawn Treader* when Lucy says the spell "to make hidden things visible," into "gold and blue and scarlet." It came to life. Fresh tendrils sprouted and curled around it luxuriantly, like the illuminated vines drawn in the margins of medieval manuscripts that gave "page" its name, *pagina* meaning "vineyard" in Latin. The abstract grew concrete. And what was the plain circle of our present life turning into, now that geometrical figure was becoming bright image? Several metaphors were available. They were the old, powerful ones people have used from time immemorial when we conceive of life surrounded by eternity, the Self surrounded by the Other, consciousness surrounded by the unconscious, in terms of one space within another. Lewis could have seen the circle as a clearing in the great forest that is always there in our imaginations, even if it's missing in the British countryside. The boundary between the two states would have been the forest edge, where we pass from the open land into the green shade of the trees.

But that would have made paradise a thicket; and though Lewis saw the greater reality of heaven as stronger and richer, and even heavier, than the fabric of this world, he did not imagine a medium that put up more resistance, that was *thicker*. On the contrary: he saw heaven as a place of delicious flow, where the stuff of existence would be more free and liquid, and all our delights would be dolphinlike. He always responded intensely to the water images in scripture. "As cold waters to a thirsty soul, so is good news from a far country." "O God . . . my soul thirsteth for thee, my flesh longeth for thee in a dry and thirsty land." "I will give unto him that is athirst of the fountain of the water of life freely." When he proposed a counterpart to Kant's go-out-of-sense-experience-and-look-back-at-it maneuver, it came out distinctly aqueous, as an invitation to seek perspective by tasting "the pure water from beyond the world." So, for the most part, when C. S. Lewis contemplated the blank circle of the philosophers, it became a splotch of greens and browns fading to the pale colors of sand at its rim, with the marine blues of endless sea around it. It became an island. Perhaps once it had been humanity's jail cell, but Jesus had "forced open a door that [had] been locked since the death of the first man," and now its boundaries were as wide open as a beach where the gulls are crying and the wind is stirring the dry grasses on the top of the dunes. It became an island; and the tide came stealing up creeks and inlets in a flood of silver to remind you, even if you were far inland, dry and stranded, that something else lay over the horizon, calling you.

Suppose you answer. The sexy airs of summer blow on your bare skin as you take the first steps off damp sand into the creaming wash of the waves as they slide up the beach. The water is cold and fresh on your shins like a promise. It drags at them too, once you have strode out to where the surf is two feet deep, three feet deep. The next wave coming in presents a smooth unbroken face like green glass, with a mobile glitter of sunlight on it, and floating cells of white foam; gratefully, arms out, you launch yourself into it and pass with a sweet, piercing shock from one medium into another. Green world, blue world, rush of bubbles across your vision, sinuous flows of water around your chest. Your head breaks through into sunlight in the rocking valley between two crests, and you strike out strongly toward the open sea. Beyond the breakwater you can no longer touch bottom, but you are not afraid, for in this sea the harder you swim the stronger you grow, and the farther out you go the better it gets. More and more completely you feel the liquid embrace of the water, and yet appetite is not quenched here by being satisfied; from happiness to happiness, from joy to joy, it grows and goes on growing. You never knew it was possible to feel like this. You never felt more like yourself, so richly aware of your senses and yet so unclouded by the confusions of them, so unclogged, so awake. You are washed clean. No secrets are hidden anymore, all desires are known. Now desire lives in you on effortlessly perfect terms with thought, and love, and justice. The best moment you ever lived before is multiplied tenfold, a hundredfold, and thousandfold. Welcome to ecstasy. "He's a hedonist at heart," says Screwtape to Wormwood, disgustedly giving the devil's-eye-view of God in *The Screwtape Letters* (1942). "All those fasts and vigils and stakes and crosses are only . . . like foam on the sea shore. Out at sea, out in His sea, there is pleasure, and more pleasure."

Lewis was always evoking ecstasy. His metaphors kept opening little, momentary windows on paradisiacal sensation as he imagined it. In fact, if Lewis's writings were your only guide to Christianity, you might think, from the extraordinary energy he poured into his metaphors of heaven, that you were required to believe all sorts of things as tenets of the religion that he had only made up as he went along, and filled with his formidable longing. The comparison of the soul in the body to a rider on a horse, for instance, suggested to him in *Miracles* (1947) that "some day we may ride bare-back, confident and rejoicing, those greater mounts, those winged, shining and world-shaking horses which perhaps even now expect us with impatience, pawing and snorting in the King's stables." Winged horses do not feature in theology, usually. But though his miniatures of heaven were so storylike in their movement, and their invention—and though Lewis's conversion to Christianity had been finally accomplished when his friend Tolkien had pointed out that the Gospels made a storylike sense—it was very important to Lewis to believe that his religion had none of the uncertainties of story. He had written his trilogy of theological science-fiction novels, *Out of the Silent Planet, Voyage to Venus,* and *That Hideous Strength,* before he came to the Narnia books in the late forties. But in his books of apologetics—defending and popularizing Christianity to a public made eager for religion again by the moral crisis of the Second World War—he thought that he was building an edifice that rested on proof. He thought he had a watertight (so to speak) guarantee of the existence of the richer state of being beyond the boundary.

After *Miracles* was published in 1947, Lewis took part in a head-to-head debate over its central argument with the philosopher Elizabeth Anscombe, at a meeting of an Oxford society called the Socratic Club. This, as Lewis's biographer A. N. Wilson describes it, was home ground for Lewis: a forum in which he regularly administered a logical trouncing to a visiting atheist, to the applause of Oxford's evangelical students. Unfortunately for him, Anscombe was not a naive nonbeliever, but an extremely sophisticated twenty-eight-year-old graduate student of Wittgenstein's who also happened to be a committed Roman Catholic, and *she* trounced *him*. Opinions vary about how traumatic Lewis found his defeat on emotional grounds. Anscombe herself doesn't remember him being particularly upset, while some of his friends talked at the time of him being brought "to the foot of the cross" by the experience. A. N. Wilson suggests, interestingly, that having the intellectual carapace of his belief stripped away in public by a powerful woman made him feel like a child caught out in a game of make-believe. It may have revived the original anger and fear his mother's death had caused in him. But the content of the debate is not in doubt. It was an argument about reason.

Lewis argued that the existence of reason in the world could not be explained as the result of natural processes. If a man with alcoholic poisoning claims that the house is full of snakes, we don't believe him, he pointed out. We identify his reasoning as defective and invalid because it emerges from the physical state of the body. Reason exists in its valid, undebased form only when we can say it is not influenced by nonrational forces, like having a high proportion of vodka in your bloodstream. Reason with a physical cause is not reason at all. Therefore true reason does not emerge from our bodies, but is a gift from beyond the frontier. Therefore there is a world beyond Nature to give such gifts. QED.

No, said Anscombe. He had misunderstood what it would mean for the natural world to furnish the causes for rational thought. If people discovered some version of the laws of cause and effect that was subtle enough and fine-grained enough to explain how each thought in someone's mind caused its successor, it would still "not show that a man's reasons were not his reasons; for a man who is explaining his reasons is not giving a causal account at all." That is, he would not be telling you how the belief *x* came about in his mind, but why he believes it. There are two different kinds of "cause," corresponding to the "how" and to the "why" of any belief, and Lewis had lumped them together, making every this-worldly factor in our thinking seem as straightforwardly destructive of reason as a brain tumor. It is perfectly possible for "human thought to be the product of a chain of natural causes," and yet not be invalidated by the standards of logic. Therefore the existence of reason does not in itself prove that anything besides Nature exists. QED.

Elizabeth Anscombe believed, herself, that beyond the natural world lay the God who created it. But until a better argument than Lewis's came along, there would be no guarantee. So far as proof was concerned, the humble silence still held good that Wittgenstein had advocated in the *Tractatus*. Whereof we cannot speak, thereof we must remain silent. Lewis, on the other hand—who in his flustered reply to Anscombe described his idea of a cause as "magical"—took a different turn after the shoot-out at the Socratic Club. With his intellectual justification gone, he asked story to hold the world beyond the circle steady. He took up a sketch he had begun in 1940 about a little girl meeting a faun in a snowy wood, and rapidly expanded it. Whereof we cannot speak, thereof we must write children's books.

Narnia, of course, was not supposed to be Heaven. It was more like an imaginary other island, farther out than ours perhaps, where longing could be briefly stabilized. What could only be longed for in this world would be possible in Narnia. Tolkien,

Lewis's friend, thought it was completely illegitimate, though as a child (as he wrote in *On Fairy Tales*) he himself had "desired dragons with a profound desire." Narnia was not built from first principles, like Middle Earth. It lacked the disciplined consistency that a "subcreation" needed to justify a green sun. Instead, it mixed together, with joyful promiscuity, everything, from a thousand sources, that had given Lewis delight.

Even as a child I was perfectly aware that *The Lion, the Witch and the Wardrobe* jumbled up stuff that I associated with different *kinds* of story. The witch was a fairy-tale villain like the Snow Queen, but when she dripped one drop of hissing liquor onto the snow, the sweet corrupting food that appeared was Turkish delight. There were talking squirrels in the wood, like Squirrel Nutkin, but also satyrs and dryads and centaurs, and when the witch's spell of perpetual winter began to crack, Father Christmas sledged through. The good beavers cooked a marmalade suet pudding for the children. Aslan was both a talking lion and something else at the same time: I already knew that the story of him being sacrificed and coming back to life was a kind of cousin of the story of Jesus. And now, rereading the seven Narnia books as I write about them, I find borrowings everywhere, of specially loved names, ideas, situations, atmospheres. Narnia is patchwork. *The Magician's Nephew* is set in E. Nesbit's Victorian London, and turns a cab horse into the Pegasus Lewis had tried to whistle up in theology. Prince Caspian is named after a sea in Central Asia, and his wicked stepmother Queen Prunaprismia is named after an elocution exercise ("Prunes and prisms, prunes and prisms"). Reepicheep is a Dumas musketeer transformed into a mouse. The lost mariners in *The Voyage of the Dawn Treader* quote Dante. Part of the plot of *The Silver Chair* is stolen from an antifascist science-fiction novel of the 1930s called *Land under England*. *The Horse and His Boy* is a pony book crossed with *The Arabian Nights*.

No wonder that Tolkien, with his carefully accumulated elvish etymologies, was scornful. And yet the Narnia books are unmistakably unified by Lewis's common delight in all the heterogeneous stuff he knocked it up from, and by the poetic (as opposed to realistic) intelligence he applied, starting with such small details as the green silk ribbon around the box of Turkish delight—whose color carries over, into an object like the work of a particularly decadent West End chocolatier, the fairy-tale sign for *venom*. Barring a few (a very few) tonal mistakes, all of Narnia is adapted in the same way to appeal directly to immediate, sensuous belief. The fabric may be thin, but it is always rich. Lewis beat out all his materials into one continuous, shivering silver leaf of story.

The author's voice in the Narnia books kindly explained things to the child reading. At the Calormene feast in *The Horse and His Boy,* for example, the characters eat "snipe stuffed with almonds and truffles, and a complicated dish made of chicken-livers and rice and raisins and nuts"—very exotic for pre-Elizabeth David Britain—and they drink "a little flagon of the sort of wine that is called 'white' though it is really yellow." It was a gorgeously certain voice, which in itself lent a wonderful solidity to Narnia's stars and sausages, so that they blazed in their spheres and swelled in their skins, but it never spoke from a position of adult detachment. There was never even the faintest flicker of a suggestion that Lewis was offering you something you could be expected to like, at your age, though he did not—the voice was as impassioned as you were. It breathed as hard as you did; it felt awe, surprise, fear, joy, and worshipfulness as much as you did; it luxuriated as you did in the idea of lying on the air like a sofa while the clouds went by beneath like sheep grazing on a big blue field. When Lewis invited you to breakfast with centaurs, or to drink a cup of fresh diamond juice from the river of fire at the bottom of the world, or to sail across a sea of silver water lilies, or to ride on Aslan's back "up windy slopes alight with gorse bushes and across the shoulders of heathery mountains and along giddy ridges and down, down, down again into wild valleys and out into acres of blue flowers"—you knew they were invitations he would have accepted willingly himself. He used the trick of uncondescending explanation, borrowed from E. Nesbit, only to involve you in perceptions you couldn't have had on your own. Which made it doubly frustrating when the book was over, and you couldn't invent any more of what you had taken part in.

Some people feel got at by the Narnia books. It isn't just that the allegory of *The Lion, the Witch and the Wardrobe* propagandizes for Christianity, or that Lewis smuggles in his prejudices against the modern world in the guise of mocking adult foolishness, so that children's laughter is enlisted in causes they don't necessarily understand. Or even that a streak of misogyny a hundred yards wide runs through the series. Every adult woman who is not a mother is an idiot, or a witch liable to turn into a giant snake; Susan is forbidden to return to Narnia because "she's interested in nothing nowadays except nylons and lipstick and invitations." It's something more continuous, and perhaps more helpless on Lewis's part. The seductive voice of the stories is also a bully, pushing you into feeling, overwhelming resistance with strong words. I was a very willing reader, but if someone had said this to me when I was eight or nine, I would instantly have known what they meant.

It was never exactly comfortable reading the Narnia books. The intensity of the experience always came accompanied, for me, by the faint aura of embarrassment that tells you that you have been taken a little too far, or that at any moment you may be. Yet I welcomed the embarrassment as a necessary part of the intensity, and as a sign of how deeply the stories penetrated my imagination. It was strongest, of course, around the figure of Aslan, the great lion who is Narnia's Christ, and consequently a fictive shadow in lion's form of our world's Christ, the Alpha and Omega of the real universe according to Lewis's belief. "'Are you there too, Sir?' said Edmund. 'I am,' said Aslan. 'But there I have another name.'" All-wise, all-good, Aslan constantly threatens to tear the fabric of Narnia when he appears. To borrow Lewis's metaphor, he is *heavier* than an imaginary country. Reading the books again as an adult, I am impressed by Lewis's tactical skill at managing (and rationing) Aslan's appearances so that they do not breach the level on which the story is to be read. "People who have not been in Narnia sometimes think that a thing cannot be good and terrible at the same time. If the children had ever thought so, they were cured of it now. For when they tried to look at Aslan's face they just caught a glimpse of the golden mane and the great, royal, solemn, overwhelming eyes; and then they found they couldn't look at him, and went all trembly."

Aslan has two distinct speaking voices. To the boys in the stories, he is stern, man-to-man and noble in an archaic way. "Rise up, Sir Peter Wolf's-Bane. And, whatever happens, never forget to wipe your sword." To the girls, he is tender and even playful. "Oh children, catch me if you can." "Speak on, dear heart." Of course, as a reader, you can be both the boys and the girls, whichever sex you are yourself, and so get Aslan both as ideal father and as something verging on ideal lover too. Of all the ten different children in the seven separate books, it is Lucy, the youngest girl, who is clearly Lewis's own surrogate in the book—the person he would like to be in relation to Aslan, confiding, enchanted, wholly unafraid. "And he was solid and real and warm and he let her kiss him and bury herself in his shining mane." But Lewis keeps returning to the situation in which guilt has to be brought to Aslan, to be judged and purged. These moments—when Edmund has to face Aslan for his treachery, and Aravis for being cruel, and Jill for making Eustace fall off a cliff, and Eustace for generally being an obnoxious, self-centered, spiteful, greedy little so-and-so with vegetarian parents to boot—these moments were at the very heart of my embarrassment. The idea of being looked at by the lion and wholly known made me feel naked.

And in the most alarming case of all, *more* than naked. When Eustace gets turned into a dragon in *The Voyage of the Dawn Treader,* the only way he can shed the dragon's hide, which recurs again and again in fiction as an image for fearfully hardened emotions, is to submit himself to Aslan's claws.

The very first tear he made was so deep that I thought it had gone right into my heart. And when he began pulling the skin off, it hurt worse than anything I've ever felt. The only thing that made me able to bear it was just the pleasure of feeling the stuff peel off. You know—if you've ever picked the scab of a sore place . . . And there was I as smooth and soft as a peeled switch and smaller than I had been. Then he caught hold of me—I didn't like that much for I was very tender underneath now that I'd no skin on—and threw me into the water.

It seemed that to meet Aslan was to consent to part of yourself maybe being discarded as a scab. I didn't think I was like Eustace, but I couldn't be sure. The books pressed a question, insistently: are you willing to be transformed? I was half-willing, unwilling, not sure if I was willing or not; not able to look away. I'm sure reading the books now (and I was sure then, though I wouldn't have put the thought into words) that there was nothing manipulative or Machiavellian about Lewis's belief in Aslan's claws. He didn't urge anything on you that he didn't think he needed himself. He truly thought he would not be chaste unless God ravished him. You could tell he was sure, that what a person needed was to be changed, turned inside out in a way you could never manage for yourself, because your fear would always prevent you from being drastic enough, cutting deep enough. Aslan the lion, God the surgeon, would show love ruthless enough to effect the cure.

The question of transformation became inescapable in the final book, *The Last Battle,* when Lewis started dismantling Narnia. (My favorites were the middle ones in the series, *The Voyage of the Dawn Treader,* and *The Silver Chair,* where Narnia was least whirled about by the turbulence of beginnings and endings.) The stars fall, the inhabitants of Narnia troop past Aslan and are divided into the saved and the damned, giant lizards eat all the trees and grass, a tidal wave drowns the bare land, and then, when the "dreary and disastrous dawn" comes up over the empty sea, Aslan says to Father Time, "Now make an end." "He took the Sun and squeezed it in his hand as you would squeeze an orange. And instantly there was total darkness." After that, there was nowhere to go but through the great Door with the characters into what Lewis presented as an even better Narnia, with a strange Platonic geometry about it that meant it got brighter and more vivid with every step into it they took, ad infinitum. This really was Heaven; and Aslan reveals to Peter, Lucy, Edmund, Eustace, Jill, Digory, and Polly that they have died in a train crash, and can stay forever. "And as He spoke, He no longer looked to them like a lion . . ."

The Last Battle upset me: I reread it far less often than the other six books. From the very beginning of the book, when Shift the Ape finds a lion skin and begins scheming to impersonate Aslan, new tones of moral failure and shoddiness are admitted into Narnia that were never allowed to be there before. Narnia suddenly becomes a world where the villainy of villains is no longer contained and demarcated by a limited story-set of emotions, but can spread out to confuse the innocent, and to taint the story's world. The destruction of Narnia begins long before the giant's hand crushes out the sun; it has already become un-Narnian by breaking the rules that tacitly governed it till then. Lewis, I think, intended the disappointment and bewilderment you feel about this as a child, reading, to make you ready to migrate out of Narnia. He wants its rather sudden corruption to lead you into endorsing his rejection of it. You are supposed to be glad that it is replaced by a better, Platonic Narnia where the apples are yet more apple-y, and old friends from the previous books appear, yet more characteristically themselves.

But the killing of Narnia remained traumatic for me because the promise of the shining land beyond the Door didn't seem very different from the promise Narnia had held out before. I thought I already had a place that would remain forever rich and full, not because it had passed into eternity, but because the story had said it was so. Lewis might have felt the need to abolish his imaginary island, but his reasons were obscure to me; and when he pushed me to choose, I found that I didn't want to go through his Door into death. In the end, I did not want to be transformed. I wanted to linger on the island, not swim out to sea.

I did experiment, sometimes, with bringing Narnia back over the line into this world. I imagined dryads in the woods at Keele, smoothing out their shining hair with birch-bark combs. My friend Bernard and I swapped Narnian trivia and called ourselves Narniologists. I scattered white rose petals in the bathtub, and took a Polaroid picture of the dinghy from my Airfix model of the *Golden Hind* floating among them, to re-create the lily sea. But I never felt I had connected to the live thing in Narnia that could send a jolt through my nerves, except once. I had the poster map of Narnia by Pauline Baynes up on the wall on the upstairs landing at home. In the top right-hand corner, she'd painted Aslan's golden face in a rosette of mane. Once, when no one was around, I crept onto the landing and kissed Aslan's nose in experimental adoration—and then fled, quivering with excited shame, because I had brought something into the real world from story's realm of infinite deniability.

CHAPTER FOUR

The Town

. ■ .

I was speeding down an unfamiliar country road, like Milo in
Norton Juster's *Phantom Tollbooth,* who assembles the purple
kiosk he received in the mail, and drives past it in his small electric car, to find himself abruptly elsewhere. Only I was not on my
way into Juster's lovely territory of paradox and logic games,
the only twentieth-century counterpart to the two kingdoms
Lewis Carroll invented for Alice. I was bound for a place where
all the riddles were concrete, and human, and sociable. I was
going, in fact, to another kind of island: an island of people in
a sea of prairie emptiness. Mile after mile, the two-lane highway unreeled across South Dakota. As we steered from a long
straight into another long, smooth curve, the big Oldsmobile
swayed liquidly on its springs. Every mile, dirt roads to the left
and right marked off the boundaries of another square field of
maize or soybeans. (From the air, when I was flying in, they had
looked like green carpet worn down till the brown backing fiber
showed through.) Every two or three miles, the prairie rose up
to a gentle crest, from which you could look forward to a new
horizon identical to the previous one. Once this was an ocean
floor. The water was gone, but the land rolled on with oceanic

sameness. Puffball clouds overhead drifted southward in inexhaustible ranks, and nothing changed, for mile after mile after mile, until we reached the town of De Smet, pronounced Dee Smett, where I was due to write a newspaper feature about Laura Ingalls Wilder, who settled here with her family in the 1880s, and fifty years later immortalized this town, among all the prairie towns of the Dakotas, in the later books of her *Little House* series. The town is small, but thanks to Laura Ingalls Wilder the number of people who have heard of it is huge. All seven of the *Little House* books appear in the list of the top thirty best-selling children's books of all time. The most popular two of them have cumulative paperback sales, in America alone, of six million copies; the others have all sold around four million.

De Smet is leafy now. The hydrophilic cottonwood trees the settlers brought with them have grown till they shade the streets of white wood-framed houses, and limit the dominion of the big sky. Main Street, which I knew from *Little Town on the Prairie* as a strip of mud and raw lumber perched on the open grassland, is old, as old goes in South Dakota, showing a century of history in its double row of buildings between the highway and the railroad line. This is an island well furnished with amenities. A town of 1,500 people in England might have a pub and post office; but it's 35 miles from De Smet to the next settlement of any size, so here there are stores and garages, a motel and a hotel, a high school and a hospital and a National Guard armory and a café called the Pie-o-neer. The wooden surveyor's cabin where the Ingalls family spent the winter of 1879 in *By the Shores of Silver Lake* has been brought into town—Silver Lake was drained—and is the headquarters of the Laura Ingalls Wilder Memorial Society. De Smet ladies in mobcaps, and De Smet girls wearing sprigged muslin, guide a steady flow of pilgrims around the Ingalls sites. It's a girly heritage, and most of the visitors are female, though not all. "We had two men looking around last week, without any women making them," say the ladies. There comes a moment on every tour, apparently, when the guides can pick the lovers of the books out from the fan club of the *Little House* TV series. "We show them the portrait of Charles Ingalls," say the ladies—and those who were expecting Laura's Pa to look like Michael Landon, with his seventies big hair and his acres of tanned muscle, see instead a plain and slightly pop-eyed Victorian gent with a spade beard. "They go, 'Oh, what? Wow!'" The tour takes in the surveyor's house, then the site of the building where the family huddled through the seven famine months of The Long Winter, and finally the comfortable Victorian home where Pa and Ma Ingalls achieved a modest prosperity in the unnarrated years after Laura Ingalls married Almanzo Wilder.

Also, the town puts on a pageant every year for Independence Day, out on the edge of the prairie beside Pa Ingalls's original homestead site. The sun goes down behind the next western swell of the prairie, and Big Slough fills up with shadow. (It's pronounced "sluff," it seems: as a child I always thought of it as a "slao.") While eager mosquitoes feed on the audience, the townspeople reenact the stories, with horse-drawn wagons, and speeches lip-synched to a prerecorded soundtrack broadcast from a big PA system. Of course, the Little House connection is an asset that the town is shrewdly exploiting. It gives De Smet an insurance against the ups and downs of the farm economy that its neighbors just don't have. But the use modern De Smet makes of its past isn't merely cynical. There is still a continuity of values you can distinguish, between the settlers who celebrated the Fourth of July here for the first time and their great-great-grandchildren who do the same, and sell their celebration as I watch in the summer of 1998. Here you still see, as you do in Laura Ingalls Wilder's books, the aboriginal American civility and idealism that belonged to Jefferson's republic of farmers and merchants.

It shows in public rituals: when the cast of the pageant sings "My Country 'Tis of Thee" on the darkening prairie, the audience spontaneously, unself-consciously joins in.

> My country, 'tis of thee,
> Sweet land of liberty,
> Of thee I sing . . .

It shows too in the manners of individuals. People in De Smet wave to passersby, presumably because, out here in what the nineteenth-century cartographers named "The Great American Desert," other people are valuable. Children wave. Women wave. Men moseying down Main Street in their pickups see a stranger waiting to cross the road and raise their hand solemnly to an imaginary hat brim. Even De Smet's teenage boys, doomed to cruise around and around the street grid at dusk for the five thirsty years between the driving age and the drinking age, set aside their raging hormones for long enough to wave at you.

After dark on Independence Day I found myself at the gas station, smoking Costa Rican cigars with the photographer assigned to the feature. Into the forecourt pulled an expensive-looking four-wheel-drive, packed with what seemed to be every female member of a large family; two generations of them, I thought, but it was bizarrely hard to tell, because from the fourteen-year-olds to the forty-year-olds, they were all dressed in the same moussed cowgirl style. Like a lot of people in a state without a city in it, they were all dressed up with absolutely nowhere to go. Night had arrived as a dismal challenge to find some entertainment: any entertainment. My, they were bored. But here was a stray Englishman! The sequence of what followed is blurred in my mind, but somehow I progressed from showing off my accent, to singing in it, to doing bunny hops between the pumps in the middle of a line of temporarily not-bored cowgirls. All of De Smet's youth had pulled their cars into the gas station too and formed a fascinated circle. The mother— if she was the mother—seemed to be urging me together with a cowgirl of about sixteen—if she was sixteen. I waved my wedding ring with increasing desperation. The photographer looked on with an expression somewhere between amused and aghast. "I've got everything I need," he said. "I think I'll hit the sack and drive outta here early tomorrow. Are you sure you're all right?" No, I wasn't sure. Being agreeable seemed to have got me, yet again in my life, into a situation of vague and many-sided embarrassment, from which I knew I was going to slink away to the motel, leaving puzzlement behind in the minds of people who had not, after all, asked me to make a dancing fool of myself. I'd volunteered. It seemed I hadn't learned De Smet's lesson too well, though I knew what it was: Be Steadfast.

Usually Americans focus on the future, and kick yesterday impatiently out of tomorrow's path. On the prairie, on the other hand, people shrewdly suspected that the past had survival value, and they were, to boot, stubborn. You had to be stubborn to stay. You had to be stubborn to go on making the farmer's bet against drought and deluge every year. I met one living relict of the Ingallses. Mr. Harvey Marx was ninety-one years old. He'd been a pallbearer in 1941 at the funeral of Grace Ingalls, Laura's youngest sister. It took me a little time to digest this information, and fit it together with the enclosed world of the stories, where the hands and faces of Pa and Ma and the girls are lit by Laura's remembering attention as if by lamplight. This was Baby Grace, who had a swan's-down hood for Christmas! He helped bury Baby Grace! Mr. Marx lived in Manchester, ten miles west, an object lesson in what happened to a prairie town that failed to thrive. Only four houses were still occupied. The Stars and Stripes was flying on Mr. Marx's lawn for Independence Day, and he had a photograph of Richard Nixon on his wall. A couple of days before I called on him, he'd checked himself and his wife, Lucille, out of the old people's home in De Smet. She needed constant nursing care, so he was providing it. "I said for better or for worse," he explained. "Now it's at the worse." You keep the past connected to the present, and to the future, by keeping your promises. The horizon was a line of endless green.

I admired Mr. Marx. But then, I expected to. He existed in a landscape that signified kept promises to me for almost three decades before I actually laid eyes on it. The books I read as a child that taught me about how people should treat each other were almost all set inside the circle drawn upon emptiness by a small community of one kind or another. Rather than being the circle of the solitary self and its experiences, beyond which lay the ineffable, or Narnia, or a philosophical empty set, this was the circle within which people were together, with loneliness all around. Though Narnia did not yet lose its power, when I was nine and ten I chose more and more stories that operated inside this circle: that took me to town. While in Narnia good and evil were distinct, as distinct as a lion is from a witch, in town they had to be worked out, in the actions of people who had to live tomorrow with what they and everybody else did today. It made vivid sense to me when I read about the society of the little town on the prairie being put together from its original elements—wood and paint, but also the rules of behavior, which are the impalpable materials of the shared life. I too was assembling bits and pieces then, putting together society for the first time. Every kid is a pioneer.

The towns in stories weren't always literal towns. The social islands of fiction take many forms. For Jane Austen, the grandmother of all novels of the shared life, it was the small world of the rural gentry, with its continual round of visits and meetings between the few families qualified to form polite society in a country district. In children's books it can be a village, it can be a one-ended road in suburbia, it can be a city block with a store or a deli that everybody uses. The similarity to the settings of soap operas isn't an accident. A soap is only a social island where the supply of events has metastasized. What matters is that the people should be willy-nilly interlocked with one another, so that the effects of what each does are felt as a pulse that propagates through the connections between them. Any sufficiently connected community of the right size will do. It has to be large enough for mutual knowledge to be incomplete, but small enough for the resulting secrets still to be powerful. Stories, soaps, and even the circles of friendship and family in our real lives, seem to settle for a clump of between ten and thirty significant players. Human beings seem to be able to hold the relationships of a group that size in our heads instinctually, perhaps because we once foraged across the savannah in troupes that big, and forever after have been most attuned to hierarchy and solidarity when they arise on the scale of that first, mobile township. Fewer than ten significant others in a life spells hermithood; many more than thirty implies they're not that significant after all, and, when reading fiction, brings you inevitably to the point where you can't remember who the person speaking is.

Children's books can find a town in a boarding school, if the author doesn't play school life entirely for laughs, as in Billy Bunter, or Molesworth, or the Jennings stories. From Angela Brazil and the Chalet School books, through to the unexpected rebirth of the genre at Hogwarts in the Harry Potter series—where a new atmosphere, both magical and democratic, still does not displace such key features as the sneering rich boy, and the contest for the house cup—school stories explore what are essentially autonomous towns of children. As a perceptive critic of Harry Potter pointed out, what makes the school setting liberating is that school rules are always arbitrary rules, externally imposed. You can break them, when you get into scrapes, without feeling any guilt, or without it affecting the loyalty to the institution that even unruly characters feel, right down from Angela Brazil to Joanne Rowling. Harry loves Hogwarts. The rules of conduct that really count are worked out by the children themselves, and exist inside the school rules like a live body inside a suit of armor. School stories are about children judging each other, deciding about each other, getting along with each other. The adults whose decisions would be emotionally decisive—parents—are deliberately absent.

In the same way, a town can sometimes be a single family, if the family is large enough, or the children alone enough, for the horizontal relationships between brothers and sisters to predominate over the vertical ones between each child and its father or mother. E. Nesbit's nonmagical stories—the *Bastable* series, *The Railway Children*—take care to remove one parent, into prison or death or a faraway country, and to interpose a surrogate, from a housekeeper to the Great Southern Railway Company, between the children and the remaining parent, to be an authority who can be upset without emotional repercussions.

From these descend all the books about children who have the skill to have very autonomous adventures, like the Swallows and Amazons, or Elizabeth Enright's confident Melendy family in 1940s New York, and all the books in which groups of children are cut off from their parents and have to live in a barn, or cope in the outback, or negotiate food and shelter in the London of the Blitz. With their emphasis on interchange and getting things done together, these are distinctly different from the stories about individual survival by children down through history, whose settings sometimes overlap: Barbara Leonie Picard's achingly unhappy *One is One,* for example, with its medieval orphan always left furthest from the fire, or Frances Hodgson Burnett's magnificently lonely *A Little Princess,* which is a combination dead parents–cruel school story. When I read these I felt a frantic identification that diverged completely, as a sensation, from the steady feeling of my curiosity expanding crisscross in all directions as it was fed on new people talking to each other.

But I was nourished most, and felt the people were most real, when the town was a real town, and above all when it was a small town in America. Laura Ingalls Wilder's De Smet; Louisa May Alcott's Concord; Tom Sawyer's Hannibal; Harper Lee's Maycomb; even the small towns in Illinois, lit by gothic flashes of lightning, to which Ray Bradbury returned (*Dandelion Wine, Something Wicked This Way Comes*) whenever he wanted to set supernatural perils in a landscape of archetypal boyhood. America was far away. I wasn't entirely sure where to find it on a globe, and I didn't quite know *when* it was either. How did the shreds of its history I was picking up align with the running order I'd put together for the British past? As the child of historians, I scorned the idea of having one big bin called "the olden days" you threw everything into. In Britain, the Romans came before the Vikings who came before William the Conqueror who came before knights in castles who came before Queen Elizabeth who came before men in wigs who came before the Victorians who came before the War against Hitler, which happened when my parents were children; and the past ended just before I was born, conveniently and miserably symbolized by them taking away steam trains. In America . . . well, George Washington was a man in a wig, so he came before the covered wagons. The Civil War that Jo March's father had gone off to be a chaplain in was completely mysterious, but *Little Women*'s emphasis on being good clearly linked up with the time of the Victorians, as did Ma's upbringing of the girls in the *Little House* books, only more remotely. Presumably the New York of the skyscrapers and the big benevolent Irish policemen came later again.

The trouble was that America seemed to have reached a state I thought of as modern, with things like cars to tell you so, a long time ago, and then to have stayed like that, showing the passing of time with subtler changes in its status quo of presidents and high schools and football games, none of which I knew how to interpret. When, for example, was this? "Somehow, it was hotter then: a black dog suffered on a summer's day; bony mules hitched to Hoover carts flicked flies in the sweltering shade of the live oaks on the square. Men's stiff collars wilted by nine in the morning. Ladies bathed before noon, after their three o'clock naps, and by nightfall were like soft teacakes with frostings of sweat and sweet talcum." I had no idea what I would have found if I had visited President Nixon's present-day America. I'd been taken into a room full of hushed, awed adults to see a white blob that was Neil Armstrong float awkwardly across a fuzz of static, which was the surface of the moon. On the other hand my cousins went to America, and a grizzly bear tried to steal their cocoa. Did Americans still listen to Victrolas? Still eat meat loaf? Still drive Pierce Arrow limousines? Still wear jackets with big letters of the alphabet on the back?

We had no TV then, by my parents' choice. Perhaps if we'd had one, a picture of America would have built up by itself in my mind—silt from the river of images in *Kojak* and *Columbo*—which at least resembled the real thing as a film set resembles reality. Instead, with a bit of help from book illustrations, I supplied my own images for screen doors and storm windows, Thanksgiving dinners and feed stores, courthouses and midwinter skating parties. I hoisted Old Glory on its pole, and blew the wind to make it flap. Often I got things wrong, because I followed my European models too closely. I always assumed in *To Kill a Mockingbird,* for example, that because Jem and Scout and Atticus lived in a town, they and all the neighbors must live in town houses, two or three stories high and joined together in a terrace. I knew that Jem had to sprint across a front yard to slap the railing of Boo Radley's house, when Dill dared him to, but I never imagined that the Radley place might have garden all around it. When I finally saw the film of the book late in my teens, with Gregory Peck as Atticus, I was astonished to see the children walking home up a kind of meandering avenue of bungalows. I felt a disorienting pang. It was the sensation of my homemade Maycomb being peeled off the armature of Newcastle-under-Lyme that I had wrapped it in, and without the familiar town beneath it to give it bulk, being revealed as papery thin, like the discarded skin of a snake. But I believed in what I visualized while I was reading, because the reality of the towns' inhabitants was palpable, and that made the places real no matter how much of the stuff in them I had to supply. Miss

Maudie Atkinson of Maycomb is a sharp-tongued, cake-baking, fanatically gardening middle-aged lady with a liberal intelligence, who never laughs at Scout Finch except when Scout means to be funny. "She had never told on us, had never played cat-and-mouse with us, she was not at all interested in our private lives. She was our friend." This solidity transfused itself into Miss Maudie's scuppernongs, whatever the hell *they* were. (I only knew that Jem and Scout were allowed to eat them.)

I learned to recognize the intense existence with which characters like Miss Maudie were endowed as something particularly American, though at ten I could not possibly have named it, for I knew nothing about American history and culture, and it grew from the sense, engrained deeply in both of them, that American life is a revolution without banners. Small towns in the United States do not fly flags exhorting their citizens to fulfill the Five Year Plan, or broadcast stirring music from loudspeakers to strengthen them while they work in the fields. The apparatus is missing that you associate with a social experiment. There is only the bank, the courthouse, the grain elevator, the railroad depot. But then the social experiment under way is the construction of a shared life from the pursuit of individual happiness. Americans often imagine that certain freedoms are uniquely their own, when in fact they are common to the citizens of every democracy. But America *is* unique in its emphasis on liberty, not as the means to some further end like social justice, but as the final and ultimate end in itself, the completion of everything that politics can do for the individual. The freedoms of speech and of assembly are valuable because they allow the individual man and woman to exercise their faculties as widely they wish, not because anything systematic might need changing. In Britain in the 1970s I grew up with the idea that elections existed so that people could make a fundamental choice every five years about how society ought to be organized. These days, of course, Britain and the rest of Western Europe have drifted a long way toward the American perception of the electoral process; but the outlines of a difference are still visible. Beneath the amazing firework displays of cash and the passionate attention to small differences between the candidates, American elections are really about selecting competent administrators, to oversee an ancient consensus. It is still an honor to meet the president, and he is guarded by chocolate-box soldiers who satisfy the Ruritanian urge that never goes away even in republics; but those are shallow, almost vestigial emotions. It is *just living* that is invested with revolutionary fervor.

In fiction, this has meant that the hopes and desires of individuals, and the connections they make among each other, tacitly carry the whole national story, which has no arena except the particular lives of particular Americans. They are full of immanent importance. A hundred and twenty years ago, Henry James listed all the things American novelists couldn't write about, because in the deconstructed landscape of American society, the institutions simply did not exist to generate some of the great standard situations of European fiction. No cathedrals, he said; no clergy, no army, no aristocracy with castles, no diplomats, no sporting gentry. "One might enumerate the items of high civilization which are absent from the texture of American life, until it should become a wonder to know what was left." Virtues that elsewhere might be celebrated in epic narratives are arranged instead in domestic ones—and then scrutinized with tender intensity as tests of the feasibility of freedom. Of course, starting long before James wrote that in 1879, and proceeding with his own very active participation, American life has compiled its own set of unique types, who inspire fictions as molded to their protagonists' social qualities as Trollope's novels were to the gallery of deans, majors, and baronets who are missing in America. Boston Brahmins; Gilded Age robber barons; Texas oilmen; film stars; the buzz-cut intelligentsia of national security; advertising men who commute from Connecticut, drink martinis, and have midlife crises; software geeks; Gen-X slackers. Social forms are constantly renewed. And in fact, there have been some institutions in America more crushingly hierarchical and determining of behavior than even the crustiest Old World drawing room: slavery, for example, and its long legacy of apartheid in the South. But the picture that characteristically emerges from American storytelling is one of people making deliberate experiments with their destinies. Compare Tom Wolfe with Balzac, the model for the social range of his fiction, or Dickens, his model of comic energy: his people are far more self-determined, more self-invented than theirs.

Or consider the sharp difference of emphasis in the great European and American novels that set out to explore the psyche of a modern, average man. Joyce made the thoughts and feelings of Leopold Bloom, his specimen Dubliner, open out into perpetuity, where experience proves to follow again and again the same ancient structures of meaning. Bloom is ordinary going on universal. Rabbit Angstrom on the other hand, the hero of John Updike's *Rabbit* novels, lives specimen days in America in the sense that he takes one specimen path through his time's possibilities for love and sex and work and betrayal. Sometimes he succeeds, sometimes he fails; his choices are exhilarating to read about in the same way that it is exhilarating for a European traveler to awaken in a Holiday Inn in

Middle America, and to draw back the curtain and look out on a parking lot struck by the morning sun, and, seeing the Turtle Waxed hoods of the cars shining in as many colors as there are in the rainbow of towels displayed in a department store, or in a paint company's catalog of shades, to realize that he is in a place devoted to the frank, practical, literal satisfaction of ordinary desires. Of course, America's array of stuff is no guarantee of happiness, just an incitement to try for it: that's what makes it exciting. The flood of things from the horn of plenty coexists with the difficulty there has always been in obtaining the inner possessions that cannot be bought, cannot be commanded. Rabbit knows himself incompletely, makes a sense of his life, which is constantly eroded by forgetting. When he dies, which he does on the page in front of us during a pickup game of basketball, the whole semi-illuminated structure of his existence slips out of sight for good, never to be known again, unless there is a God to catch the falling soul of a basketball-playing car-dealing sensualist; which Updike, a Lutheran, does not rule out. But the partiality and incompleteness of his life is what makes him typical. Rabbit is a citizen of a republic that exists only in the lives of its citizens. Rabbit is routinely unique. When the grand designs are gone, wrote Henry James, "The American knows that a good deal remains; what it is that remains—that is his secret, his joke, as one might say."

I didn't get the joke, when I was ten. But I could plot the stories of American towns against material I was familiar with. I knew that the people I met in these towns were a different proposition from the inhabitants of the funny books of fantasy I was reading at the same time, and loved just as much. I interleaved reading *The Little House* books with reading Joan Aiken's *Black Hearts in Battersea* and T. H. White's *The Sword in the*

Stone. The effect in my mind was like opening a fan made up of alternate dollar bills and peacock feathers. And the people in the fantasies were certainly different. They were already complete when you met them. Joan Aiken's heroine Dido Twite is a skinny little urchin when first encountered in Battersea in the made-up days of King James III amid her family of lugubrious oboe-playing assassins; she is bigger and taller in *Night Birds on Nantucket,* thanks to a diet of whale oil, when she foils a scheme to fire a supergun across the Atlantic at St. James's Palace; and she is a highly competent near-teenager in *The Cuckoo Tree,* when she thwarts a conspiracy to kill the king by rolling St. Paul's Cathedral down Ludgate Hill on casters. But fundamentally she is always the same, always unflappable and street-smart, always eloquent in the made-up London patois that emerged when Joan Aiken threw a dictionary of historical slang into the blender of her imagination. ("Coo," said Dido. "What a jobberknoll.") In fact, it is curiously difficult to describe her. Once you have read one of the books, so that she exists in *your* imagination, your impulse is just to point her out, in the same way that it is easier to point at Bertie Wooster than to summarize him. This is one of the signs of a great comic character. However new-minted they are, they have a secure obviousness about them that is also inexhaustible, and can be carried from context to context, giving the reader more and more of the pleasure of seeing them be themselves. It is as if they have always been there. You cannot envisage them changing. When the Wart in *The Sword in the Stone*—the young King Arthur, but he doesn't know that, and neither do you the first time you read the book—when the Wart brings Merlyn home from the great forest to be his tutor, the old enchanter, with his owl sitting on his head and owl droppings in his white beard, meets the Wart's gruff country squire of a guardian, Sir Ector, in the castle courtyard.

"Ought to have some testimonials, you know," said Sir Ector doubtfully. "It's usual."

"Testimonials," said Merlyn, holding out his hand. Instantly there were some heavy tablets in it, signed by Aristotle, a parchment signed by Hecate, and some type-written duplicates signed by the Master of Trinity . . .

"He had 'em up his sleeve," said Sir Ector wisely. "Can you do anything else?"

"Tree," said Merlyn. At once there was an enormous mulberry growing in the middle of the courtyard, with its luscious blue fruits ready to patter down.

"They do it with mirrors," said Sir Ector.

Can Merlyn be anything less than a crabbed, ideally benevolent don, adrift in time? Can Sir Ector be anything other than dim and good-hearted? Of course not. Their natures are fixed. They cannot be altered by an altering mood. (There are some moods and circumstances you simply could not place them in.) This does not mean that real emotion did not go into their creation. In inventing them, T. H. White flung all he could manage of love and all he could manage of parenthood free from the buzzing mandala of neuroses that consumed him when he was not writing. But it does mean that they do not really exist in relation to anything else in the story. What they are is not established by interaction. They stand in their setting like an actor in front of a curtain, quite independent of circumstances, and effectively invulnerable. They do not require your participation to *be,* either. Since you already know them completely, you do not have to make an effort of understanding when you read about them.

On the other hand, when I read the stories that took me to town, I had to learn about even the most simplified, or idealized, or stylized people by watching what they did. Understanding came bit by bit, and it resembled the knowledge you had of real people; and so, as with real people, you needed to pay attention to what it was kind, or generous, or honorable to conclude about their characters. They existed in relationship to each other, but also, in a way, in relationship to you. You had a kind of responsibility toward them—with no penalty, if you let them down, except that you understood less than you might have done. You could find yourself in a position like Emma at the Box Hill picnic, doing Miss Bates the injustice of judging her only by one irritating quality. You could deserve Mr. Knightley's reproof: "That was ill-done, Emma; ill-done indeed."

Oddly, though they wore bonnets and said ma'am, I could tell that the people of the town stories had much more in common with the blood-spattered gods and mortals of Greek mythology, when you found the myths in their un-nice-ified form. Roger Lancelyn Green's retellings were useless, making all their highs and lows smoothly, mildly reasonable, as if the myths were schizophrenics and he was administering a massive dose of lithium. But years earlier I'd been given Edward Blishen and Leon Garfield's *The God Beneath the Sea,* and this, and its sequel *The Golden Shadow,* put the beauty and the terror back, incomparably. Zeus sees his newborn son Hephaestus is ugly, and hurls the baby out of heaven by his ankle, to howl down the sky, a golden line lengthening from the zenith. The god of the underworld steals Persephone, and her mother Demeter wanders the world weeping for her; where she walks, the crops die, and winter grips the fields. Prometheus the Titan makes human beings from seeds in clay. He gives us fire, and Zeus sends a vulture to rip out his liver, daily.

These creatures were not individuals, as you'd find them in a novel. They were far less individual than Dido Twite. They embodied qualities: they were Power, Wisdom, Rage, Desire, and Tenderness, undiluted and unshielded, so that they glared with brightness. But they did have free will, in the most wild and catastrophic form. They acted, and the world buckled, twisted, changed shape; a touch of their hands, and they caused metamorphosis, the magical change of one thing or person into another that was usually violent, and usually irreversible. *The God Beneath the Sea* had pictures by Charles Keeping. He turned this world of savage impulses into line drawings so kinetic, so full of force, that they were on the verge of mania. I looked at the rotary explosion that was his chariot of Poseidon, drawn by the horses of the sea; I looked at the dead young men who had raced Atalanta and lost, her spears in them each surrounded by a big black blot of blood; and I believed them. We were on holiday in Greece, the heat and the smell of cloves worked their way into the stories, and my parents had just confirmed, in answer to a direct question, that my sister was going to die. I took this calmly, flattered to be trusted with such important adult stuff. Anyway, there Bridget *was,* sharp-tongued, wearing a wide straw hat, just having her fourth birthday as I was just having my seventh. But another part of me thought: all right, there is this heavy knowledge in the world, parts of the world have this cruel weight, which I see illustrated here, and that's just how it is. Deserving has nothing to do with it, any more than it has anything to do with the exultations and horrors in here. Bridget is going to die. Zeus can punish

Prometheus for doing something obviously kind and good. So what now?

On the beach, I built a long series of sand tombs modeled on the beehive tombs at Mycenae. In the book, something almost imperceptible was happening. Gradually, gradually, without a hint of apology for savagery past, the completely raw world of the book's opening, where fathers ate their children, was becoming a place where custom had an influence, where there was even a kind of contract between gods and humans. It wasn't that the gods grew any less capricious, but being worshiped involved them in policing human life. Grain upon grain, the atoms of pure force were assembling into molecules of law. This was the basis of civilization, the foundation on which everything else depended. At the end of *The Golden Shadow,* the hero Hercules rescues Prometheus from the pillar at the end of the world where he is tortured, and Zeus permits it. *The God Beneath the Sea* insists that you can't get there without the blood and the death first. They are real, so they have to be included when you build anything that stands: an ancient idea. I would meet it again and again when I was older. As a student, I had to read translations of the Greek tragedies Garfield and Blishen had drawn on, and there it was in Aeschylus's *Oresteia,* a trilogy that ecstatically transforms a blood feud into a legal case, and the Furies from avengers who rend the world into the Eumenides, the "Kindly Ones," who thicken the fabric of the shared life by giving it the dark backing of punishment for crimes. Later again, there it was in the Koran. "In retribution there is life for you, O men who have minds," God tells Mohammed: a verse whose meaning has been obscured in the West by translations that make it sound as if vengeance is what is meant: The Arabic word actually means *legal* retribution. In vendetta-racked Arabia,

God is calling attention to the larger life that becomes possible when you live in a community of laws. "One day I too will create / Beauty out of cruel weight," wrote the Russian poet Mandelstam, looking at the pillars of Notre-Dame.

But the book I'd read, by the time I was ten, that had worked as a bridge from the force of myth to the laws of the town was *Marianne Dreams,* a Puffin by Catherine Storr. Reading it over now, I'm not surprised to find that the author was a psychoanalyst. Marianne is ill. She draws to entertain herself, with a particular pencil, and at night she finds herself in the landscape of her drawings, where a house with four slightly wonky windows, and a curl of smoke from its chimney like a piglet's tail, stands on an endless plain of short grass. But she is not alone in the dream house. A boy is there, also ill in the waking world, and what she draws sets the terms of his nights. She draws him eggs to eat and a bicycle to ride. They quarrel, and in a fit of fury she blacks out the windows of the house and sets a ring of living stones to watch it. They are very phallic, with their single eye, and they are truly terrifying. Now the faint surrealism of her dreams becomes definite nightmare. Marianne cannot erase the watchers and the darkness, though she tries; she finds it is up to her to get the boy out of the trap she put him in. When I read this, I saw it bringing the unaccountable, unfair power of the gods halfway into the ordinary world. In dreams begin responsibilities, it said. Loyalties emerge from the play of impulse. The freedom of myth, where there need never be any reason for anything except I-wanted-to, is the ancestor of the freedom in stories about living together.

The ancient horrors were silent in the American towns, but the stakes were still high. It was still a world where what could happen went to the limits of life and death. Scarlet fever could still blind Laura's sister Mary, the locusts could still devour Pa's crop; bristle-chinned, reeking of green whiskey, Bob Ewell could still come at Scout and Jem Finch through the dusk with a sharpened kitchen knife; Jim really was a slave in *Huck Finn,* and Injun Joe really would kill Tom Sawyer if he caught him. The laws that governed behavior were no longer as huge and simple as the blocks of golden stone in the wall of Agamemnon's palace at Mycenae, which I climbed up, thinking of gods, the day I was seven. In the *Little House* books the rules sometimes seemed as fiddly and filigreed, instead, as the corner-whatnot Ma and the girls made to display china, with its fringes of cut paper. Sometimes it seemed ridiculous that Ma was making Laura sit still and not fidget and attend to her duties when the whole wide uncivilized intoxicating prairie began right on the other side of whatever flimsy wall they were sitting behind. You really felt Laura's sense of liberation when she got to run, or to help Pa with the harvest. But you could also tell that Ma created safety in those improvised rooms where her precious china shepherdess presided. Her rules about the proper upbringing of girls won a little place where it was safe to be a family from an environment otherwise subject to gusts of unmodified force, in the shape of storms, or Indians, or the drunk men singing in a railroad camp. They were constructive, her rules; that was why the *Little House* books were not oppressive to read, unlike the classic Victorian stories about good children, like *Little Lord Fauntleroy* and *Eric,* which made you want to set their heroes' curls on fire. In Harper Lee's Maycomb, custom was omnipresent, but the law didn't work, and Tom Robinson died on the prison farm, because the rules of equity the community claimed to live by did not correspond to the racial code they actually followed. Atticus Finch, in trying to move the darker emotions of fear and dread into the

law's daylight, was doing something that Aeschylus or Mohammed would have recognized.

In town, men didn't metamorphose into stags, girls weren't
transformed into willow trees or running water, lovers didn't
become leopards. But people did change. They led consequential lives, in a network of relationships you could never detach
them from so that they stood in front of it like an actor in front
of a curtain. They could be idealized, like Atticus Finch, or stylized, like Ma and Pa Ingalls, but they were what they were
because they acted and were acted upon. Their nature was *in
play* in each action they took. If Atticus had wavered and let the
lynch mob into the jail to get at Tom Robinson, he would not
have been the same man afterward. This was unthinkable, of
course: but unthinkable because his character forbade it, not
because such a thing was ruled out by the structure of the fictional universe he inhabited. It *could* have happened. People
could surprise you, disappoint you, show you new sides of themselves. They could change; they could even be destroyed.

All of this meant that you had to interpret the famous moral
of *To Kill a Mockingbird* very carefully. "You'll never understand someone until you get into their skin and walk around in
it," said Atticus to his daughter. But understanding someone in
the towns entailed you recognizing, first of all, that their skin
was full. There was somebody else already there, whose personality had a different grain from yours as you read about them. If
you tried to step into their skin by imagining *them* being *you,*
you learned nothing except on the level of sensation. The stim-
uli that made them wince and gasp now made you wince and
gasp too, in imagination. This kind of vicarious experience can
be very powerful. It is, for example, how nicely brought up white
children learn to imagine what it is like to be on the receiving

end of racism—how they share, to a small extent, the slow fire in the belly of an adult man, the father of children, who has just been addressed as "boy." But it still displaces the individual whose shoes, whose skin, you just borrowed. To understand somebody else's life as it feels to the person living it, you have to imagine *you* being *them,* a far harder task, for it refuses sympathy's speedy, magical wiring-together of two nervous systems. Instead, reading, you empty yourself so far as you can, and you try to subdue yourself to the material of another life, to have the horizons another life has, to enter into its separate density, which can seem as hard, at times, as for water to enter a block of solid close-grained hardwood. But fiction's access to people's unspoken thoughts made it possible; and the ultimate reward of the town was an empathy independent of liking, broader than justice, that if you had been applying to real people, as opposed to fictional ones, you might have called "respect."

My favorite of all the *Little House* books was *The Long Winter.* This story about the seven-month winter of 1880 that nearly killed the Ingallses was also the one in which the world of the series conclusively opened out, beyond the boundaries of Laura's immediate family. Laura is fourteen in *The Long Winter.* After an unseasonably early blizzard, weathered by the family in their thin-walled shanty out on their land claim outside De Smet, Pa goes to town to buy groceries. In the store he hears an old Indian predict "Heap big snow, big wind." Feeling in his bones that trouble is indeed on the way, Pa decides there and then that the family must move in off the open prairie to Main Street; and for the first time in her life Laura is living with neighbors instead of in the only house for miles around.

There had always been reminders of the wider world in the series. There was always news, there were always visitors. From the very beginning, in *Little House in the Big Woods,* Pa's fiddle brings a stream of music and song into the life of the family, keeping them connected to Yankee-Scots-Irish folk culture. Mr. Edwards, their family friend, a "Tennessee wildcat" who whoops and hollers, turns up out of the blue every so often like an envoy from the rougher side of frontier life, to chew over politics with Pa, and to flirt ever so decorously with Ma. In *On the Banks of Plum Creek,* Laura goes to school for the first time, and has her first encounter with the snooty Nellie Olson, she of the curly hair and "store-bought" clothes, who Laura will run into again in her adolescence in De Smet. As Laura's rival, Nellie is a kind of key in the lock of schoolhouse society to her, opening the door for her on the bitchy politics of best friendship among little girls. In *By the Shores of Silver Lake,* the family has taken in paying guests, giving Laura the interesting, unsettling opportunity to inspect people who had never had the benefit of Ma's upbringing, as they snore in the parlor. Above all, there has always been Laura's strong response to the wide-open land that starts just outside the door of every one of her childhood homes. She is ambivalent. She looks inward, to the zone of domestic security that Ma heroically creates wherever she unpacks her precious china shepherdess; she also yearns to be away, flying like a bird, moving westward like the free wind over the prairie grasses. Pa sees this in her and sympathizes. From time to time he has gently stretched the limits imposed by Ma's sense of propriety, and taken Laura with him to see things or do things whose energy he knows they will enjoy together. She's built haystacks with him. With him she's seen a team of men and horses working together like clockwork to build the railroad. But almost always, these different tastes of the lives outside the family have come to Laura when she is at home; or have happened when she is with Pa; or have happened to Pa, and been filtered through his storytelling when he gets home.

Now though, in *The Long Winter,* the tactics of the series change to match the family's new connectedness. You see Laura making friendships with other girls her age, you see Pa, for the first time, alone in the company of other men. You are told about things that happened when Laura wasn't there, and moreover you're told about them directly, by the author, without Pa's voice in between. You see inside the male society of the drugstore, where the menfolk of the town play checkers huddled around the stove; and there the narration calls Pa "Ingalls" or "Mr. Ingalls," for the first time ever. You get to see inside the snug backroom up the street where the Wilder brothers, Royal and Almanzo, are leading a bachelor life that contrasts scandalously with Ma's idea of good housekeeping. They eat pancakes all day long. " 'So long as we keep eating, we don't have to wash the dishes,' said Royal." So, though the gender rules are starting to bite now that Laura is growing up, and she feels funny when she automatically leaps to catch a stray ball from the baseball game the boys at school are playing, her overall feeling, and yours as you read, is one of a greatly expanded set of social possibilities, with far more to do and to know, and far more fascinatingly strange people to observe, and to try to understand. When they first move into town, Laura is frightened by the thought of all those strangers: having to speak to them, having to deal with them. It's an ordeal and an adventure to collect the spare part for Pa's mowing machine from Fuller's store. But her perception very swiftly changes. As the "blinding, smothering, scratching snow" descends, and the wind begins to howl, it becomes a dangerous journey back through the blizzard from the schoolhouse to the other buildings on Main Street, for if the line of groping children misses the small row of newly built wooden houses, "they would all have been lost on the endless prairie." School is closed. Fewer and fewer trains get through to De Smet with supplies; then none at all. The seventy-five people in town no longer look like an impossible crowd. Laura starts to think of them as possibly sheltering. They are folded, at least, into her sense that even counting the whole town, they are all frighteningly alone.

But even after Laura was warm she lay awake listening to the wind's wild tune and thinking of each little house, in town, alone in the whirling snow with not even a light from the next house shining through. And the little town was alone on the wide prairie. Town and prairie were lost in the wild storm which was neither earth nor sky, nothing but fierce winds and a blank whiteness.

Her anxiety has changed. No longer: is this too many people? But: is it enough?

Pa and Ma had not expected that the small harvest from their first summer on their prairie claim would have to feed the family through the winter without bought groceries to eke it out. But without the trains, the shops are soon empty. The town settles into a ferocious pattern of blizzards: two or three days of howling whiteness, and then one day of brilliant blue clarity, bitingly cold, that ends when the next blizzard cloud appears in the northwest. The cold has driven the prairie animals far away to the south, so that source of food is closed too. On clear days, Pa drives his sledge out of town to fetch hay from the claim, out onto snowfields wiped of every trace of human presence. "Only the wind had furrowed them in tiny wavelets, each holding its own faint line of blue shadow, and the wind was blowing a spray of snow from each smooth, hard crest." On the blizzard days, there is nothing to do but to sit and to twist hay endlessly into sticks that will serve as fuel, and to listen to the storm. It howls like an embodiment of nature's obduracy, which has thwarted the family before, but never seemed so deliberate or so malignant. It is as if the wind scouring Main Street is filled with flying elemental spirits. The eeriest moment of the book comes when Pa tries to play the storm's music on his violin. "The fiddle moaned a deep rushing undertone and wild notes flickered high above it, rising until they thinned away into nothingness, only to come wailing back, the same notes but not quite the same, as if they had been changed while out of hearing." Laura shivers: so did I reading.

The Long Winter is as rich, and as direct, in its observation of human behavior. It is one of the quiet excellences of the whole series that they tactfully register, and offer to readers who are able to notice them, far more complication in the picture of the family than they ever comment on explicitly. You can see Laura wrestling with the problem of having resentful feelings toward her all-too-perfect older sister Mary, when Mary's blindness ought to overrule all impulses toward her except compassion. (I found that problem especially sympathetic.) You can tell from Pa's pleasure in Laura's adventurous spirit that he is just slightly wistful that he doesn't have a son to share men's things with. You can tell that, though they never contradict each other except in emergencies, Pa and Ma are very different personalities. Pa is mercurial, a risk taker, someone who has to restrain his impulse always to be starting again from scratch, for the sake of the family. Ma is a homebody and a natural conservative, who has faithfully followed her man into the wilderness. Ma is afraid a lot of the time. Because of the rules she has imposed on herself, you rarely see it, but it flashes out at the rare moments when she puts her foot down—in *The Long Winter,* when Pa proposes that he should go out in the snow to look for a farmer twenty miles south of town who is rumored to have a store of wheat. "Your hauling hay is bad enough ... *You don't go hunting for that wheat.*" Pa always acquiesces at these moments. In *The Long Winter,* Laura is old enough for the first time to be included in her parents' unspoken understanding of how bad their situation is. She too is now responsible for keeping the little ones from worrying. Pa squeezes her shoulder as she manages to laugh at the funny story he has contrived to make out of the news that the railroad company has given up on the town till spring. But even this parental estimate of things is shown to be incomplete. The noticing that happens from outside the family is now important. They need an external eye to judge their situation truly. Like polar explorers who've gradually got used to eating smaller and smaller rations, they adjust to living on one small loaf a day baked by Ma from grain cracked in the coffee grinder. They—and therefore you, reading—get so absorbed in the things they do to maintain a routine, and to keep up their spirits, that they lose track. It takes Almanzo Wilder up the street— young, brave, well-fed on pancakes and unburdened by Pa's responsibilities—to look at Pa and shock you into realizing what's happening. "'I think there's folks in this town that're starving,' Almanzo stated. 'Some are getting pretty hungry, maybe,' Royal admitted, turning the pancakes. 'I said starving,' Almanzo repeated. 'Take Ingalls, there's six in his family. You notice his eyes and how thin he was?' " It is February. The crunch has come. With their own resources exhausted, the family must depend on other people. They need the town; they need help. But how?

This was a far more difficult question than I knew when I read *The Long Winter,* or than anybody knew until 1993, when the critic William Holtz published a book called *The Ghost in the Little House.* Like everyone else, I thought the books' beautiful directness was a sign of their plain, documentary truth. "This is the fifth of the true stories about Laura and her family," it said inside the cover of my Puffin paperback of *The Long Winter.* I thought that Laura the character, Laura the real historical child on the Dakota frontier, and Laura the elderly farmer's wife who wrote the books in the 1930s and '40s, were one and the same person, with no significant differences between them. It could never have been this simple really. At ten I knew already that the books were *stories,* story-shaped, with a story's deliberate pace and selected heights and depths. But I thought that Laura was so vividly present on the page—gave you such a strong sense of her shoes being full, of there being a substantial person there for you to respectfully become—because each of her thoughts and feelings had truly been thought or felt back in the 1880s. It never occurred to me that something that felt one way to read could have been created out of anything except the same emotion.

In 1993 William Holtz announced that he had studied the manuscripts of the books, and that they had effectively been ghostwritten by Rose Wilder Lane, Laura Ingalls Wilder's daughter and a highly skilled novelist in her own right. Rather than being the memories of an "untutored genius," they were the disguised handiwork of a pro. Laura-the-character was a construct. Events from the family history had been selected and combined to give the stories dramatic unity, and sometimes excised altogether. In the writing of *The Long Winter,* for example, Rose had deleted the presence of a married couple who had shared the building on Main Street with the Ingallses for those seven months, and made a hard time worse with their insufficient stoicism.

Holtz's book caused outrage. It was not the idea that particular incidents might not be trustworthy that so upset a large section of the *Little House* audience: it was the threat to the emotional authenticity of the experience each had had. There was a feeling that a promise had been made to the reader by the little girl they had first met in *Little House in the Big Woods,* and this news seemed to break it. "If you're a true Laura fan you can't stand the idea that Laura could have been for one moment dishonest," one of the ladies from the Memorial Society said to me stoutly. "I know that if Laura hadn't written those books she'd have said so." There was no room for cynicism within the books, so it would have been horrible if cynicism had gone into the making of them. Since 1993, other critics and biographers have looked at the evidence without Holtz's debunking ferocity, and a picture is building of a much more subtle and active collaboration between mother and daughter, which need not be counted as a dirty secret. If the *Little House* books are better than anything Laura wrote without Rose's help, they are also warmer and livelier and more perceptive than anything Rose wrote without Laura's input. The books are still there, undamaged, though Laura Ingalls Wilder will no longer be praised as a creator of naive art; no one will say anymore, as a critic once did, that she wrote prose "as good as bread."

But Holtz also showed that the books had been influenced by Rose's politics, which were right-wing libertarian, in the style of Ayn Rand or Robert Heinlein. Her beliefs did overlap with her mother's. Both women believed that the New Deal was an abuse of the federal government's powers, and a terrible attack on the self-reliant traditions of the frontier. Around the house, they referred to President Roosevelt as "the dictator." But Rose went much further. As a young journalist in San Francisco, she'd been a romantic socialist of the Jack London school, but by the time she returned to the family home in Missouri after a failed marriage, she thought that all taxes were theft, that social security numbers were incipiently totalitarian, and that the FBI was as bad as the Gestapo. (Oddly enough, it didn't bother her a bit when the G-men persecuted leftists during the McCarthy era.) Her vision of the revolutionary nature of American life stripped everything out of it but God, families, and the market. She interpreted it as a place where absolutely nothing should be collective except the desire to be an individualist. Even elections were dubious: they might give an imprudent majority the power to demand their neighbors' property. To her, the time when the frontier was being settled almost represented utopia. The pioneers, entirely dependent on their own labors, were the type of what Americans should be— though she herself refused to go out with any of the boys in the small town where Laura and Almanzo brought her up, on the grounds that it might've been heroic for their fathers to found the town, but only a dullard would want to stay there. To her, the essential promise of America was imbued in the life of the frontier, right down to the details of its housekeeping. (As well as her fiction, Rose wrote the world's only ideological celebration of American needlework. She saw expansive, unprecedented liberty in the Ohio Star and Log Cabin patterns of American quilts, and oppression in European patchwork, cramped by kings and communists.) And this vision shaped the books, especially the later ones in the series: not as anything as dishonorable as propaganda, but as a deep substructure of values.

Which made the Ingalls family's desperate need for a handout in *The Long Winter* extremely tricky to negotiate with dignity. Right at the beginning of the book, when the sun is still shining on the prairie, Laura and Pa look at a muskrat's house together. It is a clay mound by the edge of a prairie pool, and its walls are exceptionally thick. Pa knows that is another sign that a very hard winter is coming. Laura wonders how the muskrats know; Pa thinks that perhaps God tells them, as a kind of compensation for the muskrats not having free will, and having to build the same kind of house by instinct every year. No such protection applies to humans. "A man can build any kind of house he can think of," says Pa. "So if his house doesn't keep out the weather, that's *his* lookout; he's free and independent." The lesson is plain. The price of freedom is that no one rescues you from the consequences of your mistakes. But the great winter that follows is a climatic disaster beyond the scope of normal human preparation for the future, and pure self-reliance is not an option for the family.

When I reread *The Long Winter* now, I see the book maneuvering delicately to arrive at a picture of community that will be consistent with Pa's muskrat manifesto. It's something that's handled at the level of interpretation, for the actions by which starvation was prevented in De Smet were a matter of record, and heroic record at that. Almanzo Wilder and his friend Cap Garland went looking for the wheat raised south of town that Ma had forbidden Pa to risk his neck for. They found it, they bought it from the lonely farmer who grew it, and they sledged it back to town, all sixty bushels of it, in the treacherous clear interval between blizzards: two unmarried young men braving the wastes to bring their town enough food to get it through till spring. But the novel carefully inscribes their altruism with more specific meanings. Almanzo goes because, he tells his brother, the town will have to eat *his* precious seed wheat unless he can find a substitute. We are to note that he donates his courage to the community, and not his property. The chapter in which he decides to go is called "Free and Independent."

When the wheat reaches town, the story is not over; and here Pa becomes the hero. Mr. Loftus the storekeeper, who bankrolled Almanzo and Cap to buy the wheat, proposes to make the best return he can on his money by charging three times the dollar-and-a-quarter per bushel that the boys paid for it. An indignation meeting gathers at Fuller's Hardware. Let's go and take the wheat, says a hothead. No, says Pa, "Let's all go reason with Loftus." Taking the lead, he points out that while Loftus has a perfect right to charge what he pleases, "It works both ways." They have a perfect right never to buy another thing from him once spring comes. Loftus backs down, in the interests of conscience, and also in the longer-term interests of his business. He sells the wheat to them at cost price. Something has been achieved, civilization has been maintained when it need not have been. The men of the town have faced down the threat of losing their identities in the angry collectivity of a mob. They have reconciled their conflicting interests, long-term and short-term, hungry and greedy, by subjecting them to the give-and-take of commerce. Now that they have reached a settlement in which the atoms of self-interest form a molecule of law of the sort that Rose Wilder Lane respected, the wheat can be distributed in proportion to need. "What do you say we all get together and kind of ration it out?" suggests Pa. His share is two bushels at $1.25 a bushel. The Ingallses eat bread that night, and everybody in De Smet lives till spring.

I did not notice any of these pieces of delicate ideological filigree when I read the book as a kid. They were far outside my experience. I saw a simple story about a town that shared things in order to survive. And I was right: that is the story of *The Long Winter*. It is the inevitable story of every town. The subtle reservations and qualifications passed me by, because none of them altered the emotional sequence of the events. The Ingallses need help: Almanzo and Cap do a brave thing and scorn any payment for it: the Ingallses get help. The problem that *The Long Winter* confronts with its particular set of ideological tools is the central problem of life in any group of people bigger than the family. Every society has to sort it out somehow; every individual has to sort it out, too, as he or she grows up and looks beyond the family, from a realm where people have absolute obligations to each other, to one in which all obligations are provisional, and have to be negotiated. You can't stop being a son or a brother. But you can lose a friend, you can leave a job, you can stop being someone's lover. So the question is: how do we rely on those who are not obliged to look after us? How shall we be fed by strangers? We must be, unless we are content to live in isolation.

Rose Wilder Lane's answer was, more or less, that you do it through the market, that great contractual brokerage for different needs. At ten, I didn't notice. I didn't see the negotiations required to reconcile mutual aid with an edgy defense of being free and independent; I didn't take in the twisting path the book follows to the point where it can say "we." I only knew that it arrived there. I would always remember the songs the family sang in the face of the blizzard. The emotions in them needed no caveats. Sometimes it was individual hope that they asserted:

> When I can read my title clear
> To mansions in the skies,
> I'll bid farewell to every fear
> And wipe my weeping eyes.

Perhaps heaven is one possession you can hope to have without the free market being involved. But in the language of religious yearning, the individual flowed into the collective without any difficulty at all.

> If religion was a thing that money could buy,
> Do thy-self-a no harm,
> The rich would live and the poor would die,
> Do thy-self-a no harm.
> We're all here, we're all here!
> Do thy-self-a no harm.
> We're all here, we're all here!
> Do thy-self-a no harm!

At the worst moment of the winter, when it looks as if Almanzo and Cap have been snuffed out by the returning blizzard before they could make it back to town, Pa loses his temper with the storm, and shouts back at it. "Howl! blast you! howl! . . . We're all here safe! You can't get at us! You've tried all winter but we'll beat you yet! We'll be right here when spring comes!" I didn't care then what intricate steps had to be taken for "we" not to end at the frontier of the family: I just knew that it did not.

■   ■   ■

So from *The Long Winter* I learned about what people did and did not owe each other; and that was just one lesson among the situations to puzzle out, the voices to attend to, the intentions to plumb, that the stories of the town brought me. I even began to understand what was *not* said on the page. This was the kind of reading that can magnify your curiosity about real people, and send you back to the world better equipped to observe and to comprehend. The perceptions of fiction are transferable, when they're the fictions of the town. When novels offer you knowledge of their characters that's difficult and precious in a way that parallels the hard-won knowledge of real people, they make you more interested in the life off the page, not less. At this point in my history as a book-child, I could have been born as a different sort of reader. I might have become someone who went to the printed word believing I'd find there variants of the stuff I saw and heard with my real eyes and ears. I could have journeyed onward toward adult reading in which the knowledge of people and the knowledge of characters converged—to the enrichment of both.

But I was more dependent than I knew on the idealistic, almost didactic impulse in the stories of the American town. There, *ought* ran very close below the surface of *is*: reality was constantly being tested against the promise of American life, and judged by it. The newness of the American towns was often a powerful reinforcement to *ought,* telling you that what you saw in existence had just been brought into existence, by deliberate choices. But even when they were old, by American standards, they were still judged as if the town had been an experiment; as if what the inhabitants had allowed to develop there was a demonstration of their best efforts at a community. In the Maycomb of *To Kill a Mockingbird,* the past is an inheritance, and a very confining and omnipresent one. The respectable white families have grown so used to each other over the generations that they have become "utterly predictable" to one another. "Thus the dicta No Crawford Minds His Own Business, Every Third Merriweather Is Morbid, The Truth Is Not in the Delafields, All the Bufords Walk Like That, were simply guides to daily living . . ." Above all the great unmentioned shadow of slavery hangs over the place, inducing a mixture of fear and guilt in Maycomb's whites that issues out in acts of cruelty toward the black half of the town that they cannot even acknowledge. Yet in Maycomb, too, it is accepted that what is, is there to be examined, and to be tested against principles. And for me, pattern-minded child that I was, *ought* was the key that opened the folds and tucks of human behavior, and spread it out, and made it knowable.

Without it, I was bewildered; there seemed to be too little order. We were celebrating the octocentenary of Newcastle-under-Lyme at my school. It had been 800 years since it had been founded by some baron who built a new castle. We went in a bus to see what was left of it, a stump of masonry behind a railing on a rainy street. We also got an Octocentenary Mug each. But this history had no point to it, the way Maycomb's did; it did not bear down on the present in a way that suggested you ought to *do* anything; it was just what had happened to happen. In the same way, when I read British children's books about the shared life, I felt some crucial structure was missing. I was most puzzled by William Mayne, whose beautifully written books always observed the pattern of what was rather than the pattern of what should be. I often borrowed them from the library, because I would think from what the dust jackets said that they were going to be led by an idea. *Earthfasts,* said its blurb, was about an eighteenth-century drummer boy who marches out of a modern hillside. In *Sand,* the jacket promised, some grammar-school boys discover their very own narrow-gauge railway under the dunes that're engulfing a coastal town. And the drummer boy did march out, and they did dig out a railway, but actually the books always turned out to be very low-concept, in Hollywood terms. The big idea was always subordinated to conversation. There were no signposts, nothing to extract or to paraphrase; just exquisite observation, Mayne showing rather than telling. His novels left me, always, with the sense that more was going on than I could understand, that the fabric of his towns was all unpredictable specifics. They made me feel like Alice, at the beginning of her adventures, when she wants to get into the garden, but the door is too small for her.

What societies did I know? When I was very little, before my sister's illness separated my parents from the lives their faculty contemporaries were having, they gave parties; I could remember pushing through the crowd in our sitting room carefully, and big hands coming down to take peanuts from the bowl I was carrying. But after that, to me the university mainly meant solitary rooms I found my parents working in. My father's office in the Chancellor's Building smelled of floor polish, and the butterscotches he sucked when he was concentrating. It was a modernist box, whose glass and concrete he'd fitted out with the old desk and the heraldic panels he had brought with him from Cambridge, pouring the spirit of the history he studied into the future he believed in: the civilized welfare state that educated all its talented sons and daughters. The past flowed into the future without any break for him, because the student revolution and the counterculture had happened while his attention was elsewhere. Princess Margaret had come to a University of Keele function in 1965 or thereabouts and made a beeline for my parents, the youngest people in the room, hoping they would be groovy. "Do you know anything about pop music?" she asked. "No," they said, embarrassed. And it was true. As a teenager I would test them with pictures of Elvis, unable to believe that two people who had been young in the fifties could really fail to recognize him. I gave them clues. Memphis? No. Blue suede shoes? No. Rock 'n' roll? "Ah *yes*," said my father proudly—"the music with the very strong *beat!*" By the time I was nine and ten, and old enough to go with them to the occasional Sunday lunch given by their fellow professors, I was beginning to pick up hints that most of their colleagues saw my parents as innocents abroad, while a few, disbelieving, thought they must be secret Machiavellians, or at least manipulators. Gossip never passed through our house, that I ever heard. My parents believed in noticing intentions, not the words people actually spoke, or the unparaphraseable hints of personality trapped in the fine mesh of social particulars: attention to which is an absolute prerequisite for successful gossip.

And then there was school. I had two friends, Richard and Roger, and at break time we sometimes lay in the long grass at the edge of the playing field trying to fart at will. Well, they did, but I primly pretended not to be interested, until their cackles got too catching. But Richard and Roger played soccer most break times, so I would dodge Julie, who liked to pounce on innocent-looking kids and ask them The Question—"D'you know what *having it off* means?"—and banish my uncertainty by walking around and around the white line at the edge of the playground. Pace, pace, pace, corner; pace, pace, pace, corner, looking neither to right nor to left until the whistle blew. I abolished loneliness, I abolished school, by thinking myself into the towns I had read about. There was nothing on the playground that was half so comprehensible as the way people treated each other in the towns I read about, there was nothing I knew how to pay half so much attention to, and I told myself that reality was at fault: which was the lie that has comforted compulsive readers at least since Rousseau wrote his *Confessions,* and blamed "that trait in my character which seems so gloomy and misanthropic" on "my too loving heart . . . my too tender and affectionate nature, which find no living creatures akin to them, and so are forced to feed on fictions." I hated the playground.

CHAPTER FIVE

The Hole

■ ■ ■

"Wally," said the voice from the far corner of the dormitory, with relish, "wasn't merely fat, or even obese. He was enormous . . ." I had never heard a horror story before, and I was getting my sense of what this first one was going to be like from everybody else's anticipation, which promised a pleasurable gross-out, fear you could enjoy feeling and then put away again when you were bored with it. After all, this was reading aloud—which we could do because, at thirteen, we were the oldest boys at the choir school, and slept in a room off at the end of a corridor, where we had the informal right to talk after lights out, so long as we didn't make so much noise we forced authority to take notice of us. It was reading aloud; and everyone knows that a story delivered by voice has its meaning held within the circle created between speaker and listeners. That was how it had been before I could read, when my parents read to me, and that was how I expected it to be now, with the difference that the atmosphere that governed the story now would be the atmosphere of the dormitory.

At first, when I went away to school, my parents having discovered the miserable miles I was covering around the playground,

I had hated the way that even sleeping wasn't private. You were in bed, but the bed wasn't truly your bed, the sheets weren't your sheets. I pulled the covers over me as if they were the bedroom door I hadn't got, but it never entirely worked. The pocket of warmth you made as you curled up was still an ambiguous, only semiboundaried zone. Rustles and snuffles and coughs came from the beds four feet to the left, and four feet to the right. You could hear the world that had rung electric bells at you all day, and called you by your surname, and required you to be on your guard all the time, still going on; and though the oblivion that came when your mind's grip on your surroundings softened, and frayed, and parted, was truly private, sleep being a kingdom whose doors opened equally everywhere, it never seemed to last for more than a moment before morning came and the long cycle of the school day began again. Boarding school *was* a town of children, just like the stories said, but what the stories hadn't told me was how strange it would feel, at first, to live for weeks at a time with boys' social hierarchies omnipresent and the deep connections of family nowhere.

Now, though, three years later, I was used to it all. I had found the compensations in boarding school, from having teachers who seemed actually pleased when I knew things, to the astonishing comfort of fitting in. I had, not just a few best friends, but a role I could play. Other boys knew what I was when they saw me coming, and had a workable set of expectations about it. It turned out this town had an actual niche for someone bookish who was willing to *play* bookish, and live up to the images of cleverness that were current in our shared world of comics, and war films, and TV programs. I could be Brains in *Thunderbirds,* I could be Q in *Live and Let Die.* I could be the officer there invariably was on the escape committee at Stalag Luft 17 who wore glasses and came up with cunning plans. In short, I could be a Prof. It was a mask, but it felt as if it bore a friendly relationship to my face.

And beneath these satisfactions, I had a feeling as if a long-tied private knot had been loosened. My family's unending medical crisis had gone into lovely, unexpected remission. The prediction had been that Bridget would die by the time she was eight or so, but by chance she had survived long enough for medicine to move on. They still couldn't do anything about the cystinosis itself. Cystine crystals were still forming, an accident happening in every one of her cells. But transplant surgery had arrived, by 1975, pioneered as a solution to quite different diseases but perhaps adaptable to her problem. The doctors thought that a transplanted kidney could probably be protected by careful management from going the way of her own; maybe it would give her more life; maybe it could even give a semblance of an ordinary life. So in the year that she was eight and I was eleven, her medical notes, by now a mass of paper it took a trolley to move, were transferred to the kidney unit at Guy's Hospital, and to save time looking for a compatible kidney my father donated her one of his. He and Bridget were trundled into the operating theater together on two gurneys. They disappeared through the red rubber doors: my mother took me to spend the afternoon in a little stamp dealer's shop under Waterloo Bridge. I should have been terrified, with two of the three people I loved most going under the knife at once, but I had cultivated blind faith in doctors as an essential fear-limiting tool, and I don't remember being afraid during that long, edgy afternoon, nor noticing what my mother was feeling either. I remember the stamps. They were the ordinary predecimal British definitives, in strips, in little glassine envelopes. The Queen on them was a young woman, her black-and-white photograph an oval island on a rectangle of pale, clear color. The halfpenny stamp was orange, the penny blue, the thruppence purple.

The operation had its costs. My father's hair turned white at forty-one. The steroids they pumped into Bridget to stop her body rejecting the kidney made her bloat up, turning her abruptly from a very thin person into a very fat one, so drastic and irreversible a transformation that for the rest of her life it was hard to find more than occasional reminders of the person she had been before, in a glimpse of the back of her neck, for example, always slender even when she was most enpudgified. But it seemed to work. Suddenly, for the first time, Bridget could walk distances, and eat normal food. The crated bottles of sugar water faded out of her life, leaving nothing behind but a hatred for sweet things, and a counterbalancing taste for vicious little salad dressings, heavy on the pepper and the tabasco. Suddenly her life had no fixed expiration date anymore. The year after the transplant, she stumped to the top of a Scottish mountain. It was a small mountain, but it was a mountain. The wind on the summit blew her tartan cape around her ears, but she herself was anchored: solid enough, decisively enough there in the flesh that there was no danger of the wind blowing her away. Gravity had hold of her. I didn't have to see her anymore as thistledown, or bird bones, or a crushable paper sculpture. Something in me that had been vigilant for years, relaxed.

So my mood was more luxurious than desperate as I settled down to hear about Wally. I knew who I was in relation to the six other thirteen-year-olds in the room; I knew that I was comfortably separate from my family, without having to accuse myself deep down of running away from its insatiable needs. If Bridget didn't need propping up anymore, then I, who had scarcely done any propping, needn't feel guilty anymore. I applied a practiced negative capability to the task of enjoying the half-privacy that was available in a room that wasn't my bedroom. I stretched out in a lazy X, wedging my feet down the sides of the mattress and my hands behind my head, and listened.

Wally was enormous. But he hadn't started out that way. On the contrary. His mum and dad were fitness freaks, maniacs for flat tummies and buffed muscles. They kept Wally off milk as a baby—too fattening—and made him lift weights as a toddler, so that at the age of two he "developed a nice little cluster of muscles: triceps, biceps, pectorals . . ." The child they sent off to primary school when the time came was as lean as a greyhound; and then their comeuppance began, for Wally soon refused to spend his four hours a day in training, and began to swell. He went on swelling, and on, and on, even when they fed him nothing at home for weeks at a time, and cut off his dinner money at school. What was he eating? "Nobody knew except Wally. And perhaps the men who came to empty the school dustbins . . . It was while selecting tit-bits from the garbage that Wally caught his first rat. It struggled a little, but it tasted delicious: so much so that he took to visiting the sewer outfall on his way home . . ." After rats, pets; after pets, when Wally gets sent to hospital for observation, "the child in the next bed vanished without trace, proving they weren't very observant. How Wally did it without making a mess is a mystery." And so, humiliated beyond endurance, Wally's father began to make a plan for his disposal, a plan involving a scalpel and a cylinder of compressed air—

But at this point I wimped out, and made such a fuss that my friend in the corner had to put away *The Fifteenth Pan Book of Horror Stories* and the torch. I never did hear how Wally turned the tables and (of course) ate his parents, until I reread the story to write this book, an experience that was not so much frightening in the present tense as haunted by the memory of my gradually increasing terror at thirteen. That night, I made no conscious connections between the story and my life. I didn't say to myself, how odd, in real life fatness signifies reassurance to me, but I'm reacting to the story of this fictional lardball as if it meant the total opposite, and carries me to a place where nothing is safe. I only discovered, that night, that if you used books as other worlds, you granted them a reality you couldn't instantaneously take back just because this time you wanted to say that a story was *only* a story: false, untrue, nothing to worry about. I believed in Wally. I believed in his furtiveness, and his gross jelly of a body, and his bloodstained mouth that swallowed people. As I listened, I could feel that particular phrases from the story were being imprinted on my memory in a way that guaranteed that they would pop back into my consciousness over and over again, night after night when I was at the borders of sleep, so that the dark would have the thought of Wally in it. Sometimes, when something is going to prey on your mind, you know it there and then. Some things your mind swallows, with a helpless alacrity, just so they can be regurgitated when you least want to pay attention to them. But I'd fought against this knowledge for as long as I could because I wanted to be able to handle the story sociably; I wanted to share the unbothered group shudder. It was humiliating to feel solitary fear instead. But I couldn't help it. I was scared shitless.

It was the tone of the story that did it, as well as the events. "Wally" was a string of black jokes, like the one about the hospital not being very observant. When I look at it now, I see that the author was playing a game in line with the central premise of all horror fiction. Horror is about disproportion. It takes acts of cruelty or spite or neglect that are perfectly recognizable from the world as we know it—like Wally's parents treating their son as an exhibition piece for bodybuilding—and it amplifies them till they dominate the whole little world of the fiction, by having these ordinary causes produce extreme effects, sometimes supernatural ones. Another way of putting it is that, in horror, sins become teratogenic. This is one of those extremely precise words devised by doctors so they can discuss disturbing things in front of those afflicted by them without being understood. It means "giving birth to monsters." Wally is the monster—the belching, waddling, literal monster—that his parents give birth to because *they* are secretly monsters, in a way that would not breach the rules of suburban normality if this weren't a horror story. The central joke of the story—the one that generates all the author's subordinate jokes—is that, although a cartoon of their insanity, in the shape of Wally, has broken free of proportion and is pounding the pavements eating rats, cats, and people, the rest of suburbia is still there unaltered. Cannibalism happens amid keep-fit classes, Sunday car washing, and all the other aggressively ordinary stuff that constitutes the 'burbs. It's a nightmare on Acacia Avenue. But I didn't take this game with the setting as the slightly snobby comedy that it is. I heard the jokes as sneering demonstrations by the author that he could pack any ordinary thing with malevolence, that he could seize any aspect of the daylit world and crack it open to show monstrosity inside. I thought he thought it was funny that the whole, real world could show Wally's teeth at any moment.

Maybe none of this is comprehensible to you, and my adrenalized panic in the dormitory corresponds to nothing in your experience. If so, you're lucky. You're part of the horror genre's intended audience. You're one of those people whose minds contain little or no fear they can't bear to look at; none or little, therefore, that you can't bring to a film or to a novel, and have it roused, coaxed expertly to a crisis, and then discharged, leaving nothing behind except the pleasant afterglow of successful catharsis. You leave the cinema and think, Hmm, time for a Chicken Korma. You lay down the Stephen King, give a comfortable shrug, and *never think about it again unless you want to,* you lucky bastard. If you are like me, on the other hand, the efficient mechanism of the horror plot tugs and yanks and drags at an existing terror down deep in the substrate of your psyche, where you either cannot or will not dislodge it. It is too hard to let the story pull your fear right out into the open, where it can be worked on, resolved in the story's terms, and so purged. Instead, the story just passes it new coloring, a new stock of images, which linger, too real to be easily dismissed, because they are being lent the reality of the fear you already felt. In my case, the existing fear was the clot of black anger that I had never been able to express at the way my family's family romance had worked out, leaving all of us (I thought) so eerily fragile that rage might blow us away. I had never dared confront this emotion in its true, unambiguously self-centered form: for it was not that I was compassionately upset over Bridget's illness or the pain my mother's breaking bones caused *her.* No: I was deeply, ferociously pissed off at how the long saga of illness had thwarted *me.* But ferocious is too weak a word. My anger could have been murderous, for all I knew. It had the omnipotence of the never-acted-on. I thought if it got out it might lay waste my whole world. To save my world, I had buried it in my psyche under the heaviest slab of virtue I could lay my hands on, relying on the books I read to furnish whatever was under there with whatever it needed.

So even at thirteen, I knew that the reason I was scared wasn't that I believed Wally might come and eat *me*. In the elastic space of fiction Wally's mouth could come close to me without me being close to it. What menaced me was the *idea* of Wally—which, in its way, came closer still. Wally embodied the idea of wanting the world, not to touch, or to hold, or even to possess, but to crunch, to mash, to chew down into digestible slurry. That Wally did this by eating people was almost incidental: cannibalism is the most ancient and direct way of treating the world as all-devourable, by reclassifying flesh as meat, and after hearing "Wally" I avoided any fiction with cannibalism in it like the plague, but it was not in itself the center of my alarm. Eating here was just the image for any appetite that destroyed what it desired. For that reason, I don't think that Wally aroused my fear because he embodied any direct ambivalence of mine about Bridget's return to health, manifesting as a horror of her new size. To be sure, hope had arrived in a situation that for as long as I could remember had been grimly static, and it had arrived in the shape of a drastic physical transformation, a ballooning of the flesh. That *was* disturbing. Hope is a higher-risk state altogether than endurance; and here it was arriving inexorably, biologically, abolishing all the little private accommodations I'd made with hopelessness. But Bridget was not the only one changing just then. I heard the story of Wally when I was just on the cusp between childhood and adolescence, just beginning my own transition between one regime of appetites and another whose outlines were not at all clear to me yet. As childhood's relatively stable economy of desires started to break down in me, so did my arrangements for concealing from myself what I feared about myself.

Now the terrain inside me was shifting, loosening, faltering into motion. The things I wished for were undergoing a dizzy, hormonal enlargement. Lately on the verge of sleep in the dormitory I'd been seeing in my mind's eye the waves of a nighttime sea breaking hypnotically against a cliff, and the surge of the breakers and the pluck and flex of the web of moonlit lines on the surface of the water seemed to be stretching me out with it into a swaying sensual daze. I'd lie in the dormitory with no idea what the future would hold, knowing only that it was coming, and would contain sensations I hadn't even imagined yet. It was very exciting.

But when I heard "Wally" and felt my panic rise, I was getting a reminder that there was still this pocket of emotion in me, undischarged and unaccounted, which was also being let loose by the upheaval inside, and which might also shift into a new form influenced by the tides of hormones commencing to flow in me. I wasn't frightened of Wally as a force out there in the darkness. I was frightened, all of a sudden, that with this repressed thing come back again to blend with them, my own new appetites might prove to swallow the world. What if my wishing turned out to be teratogenic? That was the alarm I lent out to be dressed as a monstrous fat boy, a mouth that walked. I was frightened of being him. It was a fear for a moment when I didn't yet know what I was going to want, now that I wanted more; and when I was, indeed, getting bigger, and feeling the body I'd had for as long as I could remember getting ready to stretch, in all directions. The epic peckishness of true adolescence had not yet come upon me, when I would absentmindedly sit at the kitchen table at home after midnight, novel spread flat with my left hand, while I ate a bowl of cornflakes with my right, and then another, and then another, until to my vague surprise I'd reached the bottom of the family-size cornflake box, and two or three pints of milk were gone. I hadn't arrived there

yet; but already the usual boarding-school willingness to vacuum up second helpings was stepping up a gear. I remember one
lunchtime that year when the school kitchens wildly overesti-
mated a pudding, and in a carbohydrate blowout I and the whole
table of seniors ate five bowls each of chocolate sponge with
chocolate custard.

Stuffing yourself with chocolate pudding is different from
dining on a human thigh. The oceanic trances that had started
to visit me didn't feel monstrous. On the contrary; they seemed
to be aimed at the opposite of a cannibal's solipsism, the hellish
solitude that would result if you believed you were the only subject in the world, and everyone else was only an (edible) object.
It felt as if I was reaching out in them, just beginning to feel the
craving for the company of an Other so dimly defined still that I
hadn't yet imagined a face or a body for her that was any more
distinct than the whole salty sea. But Wally thrust me into the
solitude of a fear that no one else shared; and when the horrible
pictures of him biting into a squealing rat, and making the
child in the next bed vanish, visited me again, night after night
in the dormitory, they menaced me with news of an inchoate
something that wouldn't go away, that was going to go on asking
to be dealt with even when the particular imprint made on my
mind by Wally mercifully began to fade.

I wish this chapter had a different name. I wish I'd been
brave enough as a teenager to try the experiment of facing the
emotions I wanted not to have. But I wasn't. The story of my life
as a reader from thirteen onward doesn't follow one grim straight
line. It was a time of hopes and discoveries too. But when it
came to it, whenever fear presented itself to me and asked to be
addressed, I always turned back to books as the medium into
which I was used to pouring my troublesome emotions. I reburied

my fear in stories, not in stories that frightened me, but in others that seemed capacious, absorbent, open to being saturated by what you brought to them. I looked for stories hungry enough to swallow my fear. I looked for new holes to put it in.

Clues about appetite are a major goal of reading anyway, at thirteen. At my school we were all doing it. The powers that be had put me in charge of the cupboard of paperbacks that boarders were allowed to borrow, having correctly deduced that someone with the leadership qualities of a soap bubble wouldn't make a good prefect, and the first thing I learned as a librarian was that the James Bond books, once checked out, never ever came back. Every copy vanished to become somebody's private primer. The thing that made them so attractive to us at that particular age was that they led you seamlessly from the boy's stuff you had coveted last year—sports cars equipped with machine guns—on to the enticements that were just starting to figure in your fantasies, and would dominate them next year—naked odalisques painted gold, and female pilots who unzipped their flying suits from neck to crotch in one sinuous southward motion. Unlike the films, the original Ian Fleming novels fit all the diverse attractions of Bond's world together as component pieces of one vision of sexed-up, gentlemanly poise. Sean Connery as Bond showed you the Platonic ideal of a lad; Roger Moore was a burlesque smoothie; but Fleming's Bond, as well as manifesting vestigial signs of being a character with emotions, so that in *The Spy Who Loved Me* he actually fell in love with somebody, came from a pre-Suez arcadia, where an amoral, good-looking, violent, upper-class Englishman with an infinite budget upon which to lead the good life could know what exactly were the very best things to have and to do in every single area of life. If you were Bond, said *Goldfinger* and *Live and Let Die,* you would drink Bombay gin and smoke Egyptian cigarettes. You would wear a Savile Row suit and shoot the cuffs of a shirt handmade for you in Jermyn Street as you sat down in Monte Carlo to play baccarat against a countess. Your gun would be a Walther PPK: not some gross destructive cannon, as favored by vulgar American secret agents, but a suave, neat little gentleman's murdering piece, to be used against vile foreign masterminds who were usually not alpha males like yourself, but creepy wet-lipped middle-aged creatures of uncertain antecedents. Your women would be an ever-changing harem, gathered from the four corners of the late imperial world, and their names would be suggestive jokes that would reveal themselves to be really quite rude indeed if you happened to possess the bit of arcane knowledge necessary to understand them. ("Pussy Galore" was once upon a time a name that only sounded pussy-cattish to the majority of British readers. In the 1950s only a select few knew American slang.)

The shopping list went on, seductively unflagging. The version of the good life it was selling was, of course, blatantly obsolete in 1977. Britain had just been bailed out by the IMF in an unsuave, un-supercharged-six-liter-Bentley kind of a way. The Sex Pistols had just released *Never Mind the Bollocks.* The cigarettes I would start smoking three years later would be B & H, not some special blend flown in from Cairo. I do remember somebody buying a pack of black Balkan Sobranies with gold tips, and feeling very sophisticated with one in my gob, but the effect we were trying for was Roxy Music rather than *Casino Royale.* The James Bond of the novels was as defunct as Bulldog Drummond. It didn't matter: the shopping list was not for shopping from. It wasn't as if, at thirteen, with your adam's apple bobbing as you read, and the first pus-filled craters forming on the back of your neck, you really pictured yourself doing any of the things in the books. Instead, they made you a more general promise. They told you that the world you were on your way into was a world of pleasures for a male person, even if not precisely this archaic worldful. One day, you would travel fast, and women would want you to touch them. James Bond provided our first-ever tips on sexual technique. His mouth would always come down "ruthlessly" on the yielding lips of whichever lovely it was; and then his hand would descend to her left breast. Why always the left? Fleming never explained, which was typical, for the Bond books are not in fact very explicit. On the page, as on the screen when the novels were adapted, the fade followed immediately after the embrace began: which probably, at thirteen, gave you all the detail you needed to be excited, and perhaps all the detail you wanted. Female bodies had only just begun to be objects of fascination, and the rapid fade reflected your own state of soft-focus vagueness about why you were excited. You would just have to wait and see, and look out for hints in other books.

But I was finding it more and more difficult to find books I enjoyed reading. I had to browse for longer and longer in bookshops before I could settle on one that felt right, whose qualities could form a key that would fit the lock I felt myself to be just then. In the holidays, I sometimes came back from the children's library in Newcastle without a single book. I'd scoured the shelves, trying book jacket after book jacket with frustrated intentness, and all the descriptions seemed to offer me worlds I already knew to the point of exhaustion, even if I hadn't read that particular title. Suddenly the imagined worlds that had nourished me had become a set of stale permutations on predictable themes. It was more than overfamiliarity that had done this. Just the year before, I had been one of childhood's senior citizens, and consequently one of the most practiced and sophisticated consumers of its landscape of fictional possibilities, its forests and islands and towns. If you're a boy—the hormonal cascade reaches girls a year or so sooner—then at eleven or twelve you're just reaching the end of a long period during which change was steady and incremental. Your early childhood now seems remote, a few pictures and flashes of memory caught up in the legendary structure of family history. Except for these hints of your earliest selfhood, ever since you can remember you've been the same being, growing a little bit taller every year, getting shoes one size larger, going up another class at school. Not coincidentally, this steady central stretch of your childhood began when you mastered the infancy-ending clump of conservation skills, whether they are defined in the traditional Piagetian way, or as the revisionists do, in terms of a linguistic ability. Literate, with a stable set of expectations about how the world worked, you entered into what Piaget named the period of "concrete operations": when you could handle all the appearances, disappearances, inversions, substitutions, and logical transformations that stuff and people in the world go through, so long as they were presented to you in the solid form of examples, or situations. Or stories—for a mind that thinks by thinking through a sequence of things happening is going to be deeply receptive to stories' arrays of organized events. My appetite for books had had a cognitive basis.

But now, as well as becoming the most junior and fumbling possessor of a physically adult body, I was going through a cognitive change too. I had, without knowing I was approaching a limit of any kind, reached the end of the things that the children's books I cherished could tell me urgently. Not the end of the things they could tell me, full stop. Of course I hadn't read all the children's books there were, or met all the characters that children's authors had ever invented. But I had run out of discoveries that could change my imagination exigently, demandingly, as if they were news from a country that I needed to know about. The Narnia books were still there. I could look nostalgically at the pages that had given me the sensation of touching something live and electric. But the sensation was receding from the sentences that had once given me shocks; *The Silver Chair* and *The Voyage of the Dawn Treader* had no new news to give me, and so they were fading out of my repertoire of important books, reduced to the mild status of former favorites. I would have to find other stories to love.

In psychology, a moment like this is known as an "elaborative choice." When a system of knowledge reaches the saturation point in someone's mind, like my knowledge at thirteen of what books could do for me—when it is fully worked out, so all you can discover without a change are more confirming details of what you already know—there are two ways to go. You can *reformulate* the system, by altering its underlying principles, shifting its whole paradigm. Or you can *articulate* it, extending the same system sideways into new areas that can be worked out in the same way as the old ones.

To reformulate reading at thirteen, you jump to adult books. One entry point is via the classics. Amid the baffling profusion of grown-up possibilities, a reassuring sense of order adheres to the novels from the past that have already been sifted through and declared good, and conveniently assembled together, as a row of orange Penguins in a bookshop, or a dump of old Everymans discovered in a cardboard box. The country is dotted with dormant shelves full of standard editions, put together by a previous generation, and waiting for a bored thirteen-year-old to blow the dust off. Go this way, and your next move when Narnia ceases to satisfy is to *Jane Eyre.* Fiction recomplicates itself for you: you step up a whole level of complexity. Suddenly you are surrounded anew by difficulties and riches commensurate with your state of mind. From an exhausted territory, you have come to an unexplored one, where manners and intentions are all to find, just like the rules of your own new existence in your own new lurch-prone adolescent body; and here the emotions are urgent again, because the great canonical novels of courtship— Jane Austen is next—all deal with people circling warily, interestedly, as they try to figure each other out, and decide from cues of behavior like the ones real other people present to you yourself, whether this person or that is the one with whom desire and affection and trust can come together. Here, again, as you were when you first started puzzling out written language, you find yourself understanding only a fraction of what is going on, to begin with. But it is a sufficient fraction for you to follow along, fascinated, the emotional outline of what is happening, just as the fraction of words you could decipher on the first printed pages you pieced together was sufficient for the story to begin to flow, holed and gapped though it was. Grown-up emotion too, it turns out, is a robust system. You can miss a lot and still get a gist that will keep you reading; on through *Pride and Prejudice,* laughing experimentally, then confidently, at Mr. Collins; decoding Jane Austen's idea of a happy ending, and working out how she expects warm feeling, ideally, to fit inside the container that social calculations make, so that love thrives when the people who feel it are equally gentlemanly and ladylike. What then? Maybe Thomas Hardy, whose characters live in an emotional climate where storms rage, like they rage for the Brontë characters, only now a terrible fatalism is at work as well, and you watch hypnotized as a force like gravity makes things go terribly, grimly, appallingly wrong. You turn the page, and Jude finds all his children hanged in homemade nooses. Then Dickens, and a twinkling, a scintillating of moods in cities as brown as oxtail soup. Or Henry James. Or Scott Fitzgerald. Or Thomas Mann. It's a new world!

This is a distinguished, a proven, a reliable path into grown-up literature. A lot of voracious childhood readers have taken it, and turned themselves into voracious adult readers. Perhaps it works especially well for girls. Before the Victorian novel went macho at the end of the nineteenth century, it was acknowledged to be a form in which women authors excelled, and in which the exploration of female perceptions had a central and proper place. Many of the other books the world labels "great" require a woman reading them to make a kind of mental flip and pretend for the duration to be the man the narrative expects its consumer to be. The canon of classic nineteenth-century novels is different. Elizabeth Bennett, Jane Eyre, and Dorothea Brooke are not heroines a teenage girl reading sees through the eyes of men for whom they are primarily daughters, sisters, lovers. They are alternate possible selves, speaking directly to the female mind considering them, despite all the differences of history. Perversely, at least until Virago Modern Classics started rectifying the situation in the late 1970s and '80s, there were probably more easily accessible images of three-dimensional female selfhood in the traditional canon of the British novel than in a twentieth-century literature that had systematically forgotten most of its female authors. Maybe now a girl making the jump out of children's books can turn to Angela Carter and Rosamond Lehmann and Antonia White, as well as George Eliot and Charlotte Brontë.

But this solution to the elaborative choice works for boys too. And once the jump into new reading is under way, the half-understood complexities of adult novels seem far more attuned to the new bigness of attention you feel in yourself, whether you are female or male, than the stories prepared for children could ever be again. Looked back at, children's books seem to be set in a doll's house world, a small reserve where the imagination is arbitrarily prevented from engaging with more than a few small topics. There are also people, of course, for whom children's stories were never anything but a small space they weren't tempted to enter, because their entire connection with fiction began on the far side of this choice. I have friends in the word business— very literary people, people more literary than me—who only started to read as teenagers, at fourteen or fifteen or sixteen. For them, the set texts they had to read for their English O Level, or their GCSE, were the gateway to fiction. It was *The Pickwick Papers* or *The Great Gatsby* or *The Portrait of a Lady* that established their sense of what novels could be, and could do for them; a very different starting point, which grounded all their future reading in the adolescent demand to be let in on adulthood, and to be allowed to engage with all the complexity they could handle. For them, books lack the primary association with comfort that is laid down by childhood reading, and which persists at some deep level even in the psyche of those who never looked back once they had left *Swallows and Amazons* and *My Friend Flicka* behind. The foundation for their private reading was a day of revision one summer weekend just before the exams, when they sat indoors in their bedroom watching a fat bluebottle bashing itself against the window, and found that the mingled cadences and emotions and ideas of the book in front of them were settling into their minds, not as a tricky gizmo built so you could answer questions on it, but as something they owned and wanted independently: a kind of unsuspected sculpture that, amazingly, took assorted bits of reality for its material and used the patterning of them to record a richer, subtler, and more truthfully multiple comment on living than they had known was possible. When they grew up, they read Flaubert and enjoyed his palette of tonal astringencies, they read Proust with a steady delight in the gorgeous proliferation of his intelligence. But they developed almost no appetite, necessarily, for story as such. They tend not to look to fiction for veins of organized pleasure that satisfy because of their difference from experienced reality. You can spot these people when you go on holiday with them. They are the ones who feel no pull toward the thrillers in the airport bookshop, because they have packed a book of chess problems, some Lacan essays, and *Dombey and Son,* which they plan to read for the fourth time.

I tried the great books. I really did. But the elaborate verbal basketwork in which Victorian authors housed the rich perceptions they were interested in just seemed dry to someone who hoped a story would give him a jolt like a bare wire; and I gave up a few paragraphs into the copies of *Middlemarch* and *Barchester Towers* I pulled off the shelves at home. I didn't make my first acquaintance with Jane Eyre till I was in my twenties, and then I kicked myself, and wondered why I had waited so long, but the truth was that at the age other book-children were finding Charlotte Brontë, I refused to believe that anything as ceremonious as Victorian prose seemed to me to be could contain anything worth having. So I ventured out among the modern novels in the adult section of the library: I had a few successes, like John le Carré, but I was baffled by the protocol that governed most of the books. Take something as simple as the titles.

If a children's book was called *The Blue Hawk,* it would have a hawk that was blue in it, with claws and wings and wild raptor eyes. If it was called *The Perilous Descent* you could count on it being about a descent that was perilous: two World War Two airmen stranded on a sandbank fall through a hole into an underground passage, and go down and down and down, through shafts and chasms, until they land by parachute in a subterranean country peopled by the descendants of shipwrecked refugees. Perfectly straightforward. Adult authors, on the other hand, seemed to be constitutionally incapable of giving a book a truthful name. Try *The Middle of the Journey,* and you got a bunch of academics in New York State sitting around and talking to each other. Did they set off for anywhere? They did not. *The Centaur* did not contain a centaur: it turned out to be just some bloody metaphor.

And I was equally puzzled by the strange silence of the authors about their characters. Oh, they *described* them, all right—but who was good? Who was bad? What was I supposed to think about them? I was used to the structure of a fictional world being a structure of judgments, an edifice built to provide you with a moral experience in exactly the same way that it brought you tastes, smells, and sights. I expected to be guided. I thought that reading was intrinsically a bargain in which you turned off your own powers of judgment and let the author's take over, so he or she could show you a pattern made by the interplay of some people who were exactly what the author said they were. The point of stories to me was that people could be decisively known in them. The author's special intimacy with them unmasked them for the reader; or rather, turned them so that you saw exactly the moral facets of them that the story needed. Suddenly, instead, I was finding myself in written worlds that asked me to work the characters out as I would have worked out real, interesting strangers I happened to come across. But I didn't study strangers. That was why I read books! Compared to the books I was used to, and was growing out of, grown-up literature seemed spectacularly open-ended. I would read a few pages, and there would seem to be no edges and limits to what was going on; no sense of an evolving shape, and so no urgency, and no particular reason to read on. Of course, the reformulating jump into adult fiction consists exactly of a retuning of your reading mind to those subtler, wider, but still ultimately decisive cues to meaning that a writer for adults constructs in the expectation that the person reading will bring an active, participatory judgment to the task. No book is truly open-ended. Ask any deconstructionist: they'll tell you that a fictional text, however wide it spreads its net, is a closed system within which possible interpretations are carefully limited and managed. But there is still a great difference in sensation, for the reader, between a story that is explicitly story-shaped, following visible and external rules like the rule of a happy ending, and one that takes advantage of the novel's great freedom to flow into any form at all that embodies the author's sense of the internal order of his or her material. I was not yet willing, or able, to *see* the ad hoc shapes of adult novels. I still needed the given forms, the definite outlines of children's books.

So for now, when the elaborative choice was offered to me, I took articulation. This meant I asked for my reading to extend to new subjects without it changing its nature. I looked for books that used familiar means to talk about new things. The pickings were thin. If I had been growing up ten years later, I would have had far more choices. In the 1980s, a whole booming publisher's category appeared of writing specifically aimed at teenagers—books designed to lead "young adults" gently out of children's books by offering them the certainties of a children's book's narration, but applied to the lives of those who had entered the Age of Acne. I could have read Cynthia Voigt's extraordinarily tough, and sparely beautiful, series of novels about the Tillermans, a poor white family growing up in the Tidewater backcountry around the Chesapeake Bay. Or the New Zealand novelist Margaret Mahy's terrific Brontëesque supernatural thrillers, *The Changeover*, *The Haunting*, and *The Tricksters*. Mahy did family life with an elegant, witty realism that made you feel you were getting a leg up to being an altogether more noticing kind of person; simultaneously, she understood how inchoately sexy magic is, at a point in your life when real sex is still three wishes away, and gleams with as much mixed fascination and alarm as if it were truly a spell. Will it turn you inside out? Will it steal you away from yourself? Or if I had been a nineties teenager, and wanted fiction to carry me through the complications of a world where brown heroin is easily available in secondary schools, I could have turned to Melvin Burgess's *Junk*.

Instead, I mostly made do with books of adventure which, like the James Bond novels, existed in a masculine blur between boyhood and adulthood. I read books for boys with adult male heroes whose thoughts contained nothing a thirteen-year-old couldn't recognize, like Lawrence Durrell's espionage novel *White Eagles over Serbia*; I read books theoretically for grownups that nonetheless showed adult men doing things that were perfectly intelligible in the context of an all-male boarding school, like escaping from Colditz. It was a bit too late for Biggles. His adventures with Ginger and Algy displayed a hopeless lack of savoir faire. You couldn't believe he was an adult, even a drastically censored one. But he had meatier successors in the numerous cheap reads devoted to Battle of Britain fighter pilots and the like. Them you saw whizzing away from the airfield in their sports cars for a date with some dishy WAAF. There was also a German novelist called H. H. Kirst whose books put you in a kind of counterpart wartime world on the other side, a cheerfully sleazy place populated by Wehrmacht conscripts called Rudi who were always on the scrounge for a stein of beer, a warm place to sleep, and a barmaid with a plunging neckline. My contemporaries who liked their military adventures nastier read Sven Hassel. Remember him? His books were called things like *Blitzfreeze,* and they always had a haggard Kraut with mad staring eyes on the cover.

Now and again the lightning struck, and I chanced on a proper adult novel that spoke to me successfully. Satires worked, in particular. When an author sets out to make you feel the horrified pleasure of recognizing a quality in people taken to its satirical limit, he or she devises an emotional path through the novel for the reader to take that is analogous to the signposted experience a children's book offers. I found *Brave New World* and *1984* instinctively familiar. I knew nothing about the cinemagoing, eugenics-believing, hormone-fixated prewar scene that Aldous Huxley was extrapolating into his satirical future, and Orwell was introducing me to totalitarianism for the first time, even as he was carrying it to the point of all-dominating satiric completeness. But I knew where I was in relation to this sort of writing. I knew that both authors would stand me where I needed to be to see what they wanted me to see. I opened *1984* and read: "It was a bright cold day in April and all the clocks were striking thirteen . . ." Ah, I thought, now you're talking. As I read the famous, exhilaratingly grim final paragraph, where

Winston Smith, post-torture, post-rats, begins to cry with joy as he hears news of another meaningless victory on the radio, I felt myself being led by Orwell through an exact, deliberate sequence of sensations: repulsion, fascination, and an undeniable, almost mathematical pleasure at the ultimate demonstration that there is no hope at all. "Forty years it had taken him to learn what kind of smile was hidden beneath the dark moustache ... But it was all right, everything was all right, the struggle was finished. He had won the victory over himself. He loved Big Brother." That moment fits the novel like a black crown, and it works because it induces exactly what Orwell intended it should.

I did also find some treasures as I gleaned the increasingly barren field of books "for older children." *Emma Tupper's Diary,* for instance, by Peter Dickinson, the author of the *Changes* trilogy, filmed for children's TV with a title sequence my generation often remembers because it spooked them and they don't know why: the one where the train freezes in the cutting. Outwardly, *Emma Tupper* conformed to the laws of adventure. It had dinosaurs in a Scottish loch, and a submarine invented by an eccentric Victorian scientist. But it actually focused to a greater extent on someone learning the laws of an alien social landscape. The Emma of the title, a stolid outsider of about my age, goes to stay for the summer with a family of near-adult Scots aristocrats, who as lairds of their glen are indulged in their play with dangerous adult toys. Show-offs and fantasists all, they tease and partly include Emma. She observes them, likes them, works them out in her head, and notices when their jokes "contain cruel little crumbs of something else, like sand in lettuce." I thought much more about the Macandrews and the way they talked than about the dinosaurs, when I finished that. And then

I loved Jane Gardam's *A Long Way from Verona,* a hectic novel about a schoolgirl growing up in a Tyneside vicarage during the war. It was the first first-person novel I read that really used someone's individual speaking voice for humor, and to suffuse a chain of events with someone's character, rather than just to create a faux document, which historical novels for children did, a lot. It exploited the subtleties—hidden in plain sight—of how people say what they say; and what they don't say.

The point is this—in three parts. Tripartite. Viz:

1. I am not quite normal
2. I am not very popular
3. I am able to tell what people are thinking.

And I might add

4. I am terribly bad at keeping quiet when I have something on my mind

because

5. I ABSOLUTELY ALWAYS AND INVARIABLY TELL THE TRUTH.

Jessica Vye, Jane Gardam's heroine, perpetually disconcerts teachers, and falls for a hopelessly unsuitable posh Rupert Brooke look-alike. She "winds" up her friends by taking everything terribly seriously. She is afflicted by embarrassment as powerful as physical fear. I found her voice incredibly sympathetic. I'd wanted to be in books myself before, but she was the first character in fiction I strongly wanted to be real, and in the world with me, so I could know her. Like *Emma Tupper,*

A Long Way From Verona carried me half into the adult world of open-ended unguided curiosity about people, along a path that I could manage. Not coincidentally, both books had thirteen-year-old heroines: the same age as me. For both of them, and for the reality of their lives, I felt a preromantic glow that was the ancestor of my blissed-out later astonishment that the girls I had crushes on moved through the world sitting on chairs and brushing their teeth just as I did, as if they had no idea what goddesses they were, what charged and roseate possibility surrounded their every action. Personhood and girlhood at once!

But despite these occasional hits I still had to search longer and longer in libraries to find any book I wanted to read. The sheer quantities of stuff I seemed to have to turn over now before anything appealed reminded me of the description of Marie Curie discovering radium that I'd read years before in an old children's biography of her. Having deduced that there was a faint trace of radioactivity in an industrial by-product called pitchblende, she arranged to have several factories' output of this stuff delivered to her in a disused Paris coal yard. Then she stirred the pitchblende in a giant vat: ton after ton after ton of black sludge, just to isolate one gleaming gram of radium.

Then, a godsend: I discovered science fiction. In a way, of course, all genre writing is a natural counterpart to the controlled world of children's fiction. Pick up a romance, a Western, a thriller, a Wodehouse comedy, a horror novel, or a detective story, and you know in advance what sort of synthetic experience you are about to be offered. Genre writers are in the business of delivering sensations for which their readers have already at least half formed a wish. They even return you to the old convention that titles of books should be descriptive, or, more than that, are contracts, which the author breaks at his or her peril. (*Leave It to Psmith* will contain a character called Psmith; there are sure to be literal lambs at some point in *The Silence of the Lambs,* whatever further resonance they then have there as a metaphor; *Murder on the Orient Express* is absolutely guaranteed to feature transportation by rail in the direction of Constantinople.) So perhaps I could have found equal satisfaction in another genre's style of predictable pleasures, although it was in fact reading science-fiction Puffins "for older children," like John Christopher's *Tripods* trilogy and *Citizen of the Galaxy* by Robert Heinlein, that gave me the end of a thread I could follow out of the impasse of nothing-to-read. Heinlein's "juveniles"—as his kids' books were labeled without much regard to the dignity of their readers—led me to the rest of his output, on the adult SF shelves in the library; first in the public library in Staffordshire during the school holidays, and a little later, when I was fourteen and fifteen and had moved to boarding school in London, in one of Westminster City Council's old branch libraries, off Great Peter Street. This was an old-fashioned temple of public reading. Tramps snoozed in the reference room. Tired globe lamps filled the main hall with an oily yellow light that made it feel as if it were always a winter dusk outside, even in June. I picked one after another of the yellow SF hardbacks published by Gollancz off the shelves. I had the whole of SF's history since its pulp heyday in the 1940s to catch up on—Heinlein and Asimov, Ray Bradbury and Arthur C. Clarke, André Norton and James Blish. The written world had been reseeded with novelty. Possibility had come sweeping back.

The best description I've ever found of the elation I felt is Wordsworth's little hymn of thanksgiving in *The Prelude* for the pulp he'd read at the same age, two hundred years earlier.

Ye dreamers, then,
Forgers of lawless tales! we bless you then,
Impostors, drivellers, dotards, as the ape
Philosophy will call you: then we feel
With what, and how great might ye are in league,
Who make our wish, our power, our thought a deed,
An empire, a possession,—ye whom time
And seasons serve; all Faculties; to whom
Earth crouches, the elements are potter's clay,
Space like a heaven filled up with northern lights,
Here, nowhere, there, and everywhere at once.

Wordsworth, naturally, was not reading SF. In the 1780s, teenage literary popcorn came in the shape of cheap romances and nutty gothics, books in which young men chanced on gigantic diamonds or mad monks cackled in dungeons extending ad infinitum, like a hall of mirrors designed by Piranesi. But the quality that makes a teenager want to give thanks is common to the genre fiction of Wordsworth's time and mine alike.

Maybe "the ape Philosophy"—meaning every scornfully rational adult voice you really didn't want to hear just then— was right, and a lot of the books you responded to vividly *were* bad; were drivel, were cheap, were "lawless." (An irony, that last accusation: "lawless" genre books often obey unrealistically reliable rules.) If I had looked at the stuff I was reading with a hard critical eye, I would have had to agree. Some of it was frankly bad. Some of it was good on one point only—one idea, one invention—and the whole of the rest of the novel existed only as a scaffolding to hold that one good thing in place. And some of it was "good" in a purely efficient way, because it worked out a daft premise sleekly. So what. Who cares. Good books are so often committed to self-denial of one sort or another. They make their fictional world real by making it austere; they hammer invented events into proportion, and subdue them with probabilities. At other times in your life, discovering limits and feeling out the dimensions of reality can be one of the most liberating things fiction can do for you; it can be an aid to a bold, exploratory recognition of yourself. But when you're fourteen the dimensions of your own character that you will ultimately have to get used to, and respect, are hopelessly unclear, while the restrictions imposed on your life are all too apparent. Sensible, probable books keep sending you back where you came from. It's the wild and tacky ones that let you see further into the world you do not yet know. It's the books that dispense with rigor and proportion that let your imagination billow out, and go exploring. They give you time, space, empire, power; an existence answerable to your wishes as your own really is not. Their freedom from what really is becomes your freedom, very directly. They give you scope.

Sometimes that scope is manifested in larger-than-life heroics. SF is rich in characters who have superlative talents, or who find themselves at the hinge of galaxy-changing events, where one action of theirs can sway the fate of billions. This leg up to demigodhood is very attractive at fourteen. When you don't feel certain yet that you securely possess even an ordinary power of self-determination, the idea of extraordinary powers calls strongly. You know that it is a crude fantasy to dream of being the Chosen One, the unknown heir to the throne of the stars, the warrior student in the high-tech dojo who moves with a lethal grace no one has seen before. But it has a crude sweetness, nonetheless. It briefly drenches your view of yourself in welcome syrup. You are trying out the sensation of exceeding the scope of an ordinary adult by the same margin by which you presently fall short of it. In a sense, even, it's easier, at this time, to imagine yourself as a hero than as an adult; easier to imagine yourself being autonomous in the drastically total way that a hero is, when the person you find yourself to be when you put down the book is still (to use Julian Barnes's description of adolescence) "a creature part willing, part consenting, part chosen for." Wordsworth did the same thing sometimes. He read Milton and Shakespeare when he was molding his destiny as a poet, but he read Du Bartas when he wanted to imagine being the finest swordsman in all France. I read *Rocket Ship Galileo* when I wanted to imagine building a spacecraft in my back garden, and blasting off to fight the Nazis on the moon. Is this just a return of an infantile wish for omnipotence? The bawling toddler's demand to be king or queen of everything? Not quite; something from early in our history has come around again, but its meaning is different now in its new context, at this place further up on the rising spiral of development. The emergent powers that are being glimpsed in the shadowplay of fiction are a different set, this time around.

And simple identification with heroes is only one thing that SF gives, and perhaps not a very important one. George Lucas famously constructed *Stars Wars* on the theory that science fiction is just mythology in modern dress. Luke Skywalker is just a new incarnation of an ancient and universal hero, as analyzed by Lucas's anthropological guru Joseph Campbell. The light saber updates the hero's archetypal sword. R2-D2 and C-3PO are the hero's equally inevitable funny friends, turned android. Of course, Lucas must be partly right, and not just because the millions he took at the box office are experimental confirmation. In part the move from childhood reading to SF is easy because SF holds to ancient laws of plot, already deeply engrained in you. I discovered very quickly as I read my first few SF novels that mostly, when you thought of them reduced down to their emotional basics, the stories of the books were familiar. They used situations that were as old as storytelling. Heinlein's *Citizen of the Galaxy* began in a slave market on the planet Sargon, but it told the story about the orphan who finds his place in the world after many wanderings. *The Rebel of Rhada,* a novel about a primitive far future, essentially transposed into it the story of the faithful knight who saves the infant king from his treacherous regents, and marries the princess who has helped him in his adventures. And indeed, as in myth—or fairy tale— the appeal of these situations did not depend on subtle individual characterization, or on them securing your assent to challenging emotional logic. They were strong, and simple, and instantly intelligible.

Yet when I picked up *The Rebel of Rhada,* I didn't think, ah, how familiar. It was a grim, peculiar book that fascinated me. I never met anyone else who had even heard of it. The author, Robert Gilman, took the traditional Fall-of-the-Galactic-Empire scenario (another idea so elderly it had practically grown a long white beard), and imagined the dark ages afterward, as they might be if the empire's starships were effectively indestructible, and could be used by a Charlemagne trying to put the whole thing back together without any more than the faintest gleam of understanding of how anything worked, or how far apart the stars were. The plot was nothing special but Gilman made the barbarousness of his story sensually vivid and specific: it was there in walls crusted with salt, and soldiers being called "warmen," and in kilometer-long vessels glowing in the night sky being used to drop heavy stones on enemies, and in the songs of harpers and in chants that preserved garbled remnants of science. He made me see the steel and glass of modern cities becoming indescribably old, and settling into the ground forgotten; and New York becoming a fort on a mound at the mouth of the Hudson piled deeper with layers of ruins than Troy. Because I read his book, I felt the vertigo of centuries yet to come. He put new pictures in my mind, spiked and rusty, loud with war, cracked like old concrete. None of this had anything to do with being universal like myth; perpetually rerunning Gilgamesh with lasers.

If George Lucas is right, then for most written SF (as opposed to film), he's right in a way that is beside the point. Much SF uses simple and time-honored plots, not because they are the ones that have a permanent place in humanity's vocabulary of emotions, but because the emotional situation in a science-fiction novel is not necessarily the center of attention. Far from calling you urgently to identify with a hero, they're often cool or cold, emotionally speaking, offering you instead a kinetic barrage of images. *The Rebel of Rhada,* page one. I read: "The interior of the great vessel was close and smoky, for the only light came from gymballed torches and lamps. Once there had been light without fire, but the life-support systems had failed time out of mind. Deep in the hull the chambers housing the inoperative systems were stables for the muttering war mares." A starship lit by flaming torches! I thought: Can you *do* this? Is this *allowed?*

What *The Rebel of Rhada* produced in me was a composite sensation that could not be reduced to any single one of its elements. It was plot plus tone plus ideas plus visuals; it was the cumulation of the thought of immense power being used clumsily, and ignorant armies clashing by night, and Gilman's atmospheric voice, and the fragmentary quotations he put at the head of every chapter to give you the sense of a culture of incomprehensible shards. C. S. Lewis wrote in an essay about his boyhood pleasure in "Redskinnery," a fused amalgam of American Indian-ness he had found in *The Last of the Mohicans* and knew could be distinguished entirely in mood from other fusions in books that offered a superficially similar kind of danger and adventure, like pirate-ness, or quest-ness. This was the same phenomenon, except that in science fiction there was the possibility of a completely new fused experience every time. It changed like a kaleidoscope. Whenever you read Robert Heinlein, you were listening to the patter of a pink-cheeked, fresh-faced snake-oil salesman from St. Louis, with a slide rule in his pocket, who promised to lift you from the Midwest to the Milky Way for a mere five dollars down: it was as if one of the talents of Mark Twain had got away and made a new career on its own. Whenever you read Arthur C. Clarke, you got plain carpentry and sublime views. In SF, a kind of combinatorial explosion took place. The genre's freedom from the tyranny of probability applied to all of the pieces it was built from.

After all, these were stories about imaginary people in imaginary places in imaginary times. Any degree of strangeness that the author could carry through was allowed, or any combination of strangeness with familiarity. And fiction's looseness in space for the reader was now enacted for real space, outer space, the stars-and-planets kind. Where the emotional core of the plot was genuinely involving, and you felt strong identification with a character, you still had the usual freedom to choose your perspective, and to put yourself into the flexible domain of fiction as a floating, bodiless dot of attention. In those cases (perhaps the majority) where the story only needed to work well enough on an emotional level for you to assent to it, the spatial possibilities went wild. All bets were open. Your attention could be focused inside a virus, diffused through the pulsing traffic flows of a city, expanded to the size of a nebula. You could loop your attention between future and past, not once but several times in a complex knot, as you explored the paradoxes of time travel. You could treat an idea as a presence more significant than any character. You could be enfolded by forms as insubstantial as the aurora borealis is, in Wordsworth's metaphor for the light show his reading mounted in his mind. Curtains of colored air rippled constantly into new geometries as I read: I was here, nowhere, there, and everywhere at once.

At its limit, the genre approached the condition, stranger than it first sounds, of telling stories about something other than people. In some SF short stories—from the "Golden Age" of the forties in particular—the humans were there only as furniture for an interesting notion in celestial mechanics. Space opera, with its numerical overload of stars and battle fleets, might as well have represented its casts with circles and arrows. Grandeur shrank people too. The cylindrical alien spacecraft five miles long in Clarke's *Rendezvous with Rama* got more of the author's care than any of that book's characters—its almost vestigial characters. And when geological time, or cosmological time, was brought in, humans vanished altogether, abolished by the scale. Perhaps the sensation of considering human life from a million-year perspective should be counted as one of SF's cognitive trophies. It's analogous to the humbling change of reference points brought on by considering evolutionary history, and realizing how many millennia of indifferent natural processes produced the little solipsistic bubble of human society, which mistakes its concerns for the agenda of the universe.

Piaget supplies a rationale for reading stories with such an abstract payoff at this particular stage in your life. It is, he says, the era when you master the last elements of adult rationality by learning to deal with ideas in the abstract. You no longer need logical operations like class inclusion to be clothed in the flesh of examples. At eight, in your time of "concrete operations," if you had been set a problem involving ten car owners, you might have pictured them, been curious about them, given them ten different noses and a scattering of flared trousers. Now you know that all that is irrelevant; you just think "ten owners," or even $10x$. You can see through the differences and irregularities of cases to the unchanging principle beneath, the bare grid of the idea they have in common, and the exercise of this new power is, of course, pleasurable. It makes the world a giant step more graspable—more yours.

In practice, though, I avoided SF that dealt out aeons like pennies. For me a kind of balance had to be maintained between ideas and emotions. A novel could be as inhuman as it liked in terms of what interested it about a situation, but it had to maintain something like the familiar human scale where time was concerned. If hundreds of thousands of years began to pass— as in the great original of all such stories, Wells's *Time Machine,* where the traveler watches the last creature on Earth die under a dim red sun on a featureless beach that had once been Richmond Hill—then for me, some necessary acknowledgment was crushed of what size I was, reading. The idea that stories like that realized more pressingly than they realized any of their characters was the idea of death. They brought me all too directly into the presence of the gap through which the world is sucked away, the hole in the air into which everything created, fictional and real, would vanish in time: babies, bathwater, my sister, and finally, unimaginably, myself.

■ ■ ■

None of these books, though, made me *yearn* as Narnia had done. Although the passionate desire to be in the world of the book had faded out of the stories that originally inspired it in me, it remained my most coveted emotion—my definition of the best thing that reading could give. SF interested me, entertained me, occasionally frightened me. Sometimes it ran a rivulet of true wonder through me. Ray Bradbury, his rhythms mercurial, twirling the shivelights and shadowtackle of the vocabulary that made him the Gerard Manley Hopkins of science fiction, showed me a crystal house by a red canal, in *The Martian Chronicles*; in *Fahrenheit 451,* a wall-sized TV that sweetly sings inanities all day long, like a giant seashell with the whole ocean of commerce resounding inside it. I did not, though, think, "This is what I needed without knowing it, this has sent me a message from an unsuspected address inside me, this is where a part of me is going to be living for a while." But since the late 1960s, another generation of SF writers had come along to supplement the pulp pantheon of Heinlein, Asimov, Clarke, Blish, and Bradbury, and they were much more ambitious than their predecessors about things like characterization. One of them was Ursula Le Guin, who I'd known as the author of the *Earthsea* trilogy for children: excellent, resonant books but in the second rank of favorites for me at the time because of my preference for other worlds that connected to this one through accessible doors. Back at home from school the summer I was fifteen, and poking about as ever in the Newcastle town library, I stumbled across her novel *The Left Hand of Darkness* in the adult SF section. Plain library binding, no dust jacket, no clues to the contents.

I remember waiting in the rain for the same old bus up the hill to the university, feeling a mild replete satisfaction that the problem of what to read was taken care of for the next twenty-four hours. What a geological age had passed, I thought with a consciously adult air, since I made the same journey as a seven-year-old, and how completely different I was, now that I stood six feet tall, wore a flapping greatcoat from Oxfam, and had a collarbone like a swallowed coat hanger. The bus came in, a green Potteries Motor Transport single-decker; I folded myself into a seat at the back, over the wheel arch. As the engine restarted, the judder in the chassis transmitted itself up my legs, and incited a rat-a-tat-tat shake in my knees, which I ignored. Recently, while this new body of mine was bedding itself in, I'd got used to a whole class of spasmodic buzzings and flutterings and twitchings. The new nerves would fire on their own, and a shiver would convulse my shoulders, or my heels would drum on the ground in the same spasm—called "clonus"— that dancers in Java, apparently, use in order to oscillate faster than you can choose to do consciously. Also, my blood did not seem to have got completely used to the longer distances it had to travel around me. If I stood up suddenly, it drained out of my head, and my vision went with it for a moment or two, replaced by a pulsing weave of cream-and-gray squiggles, like the abstract pattern on a not-very-attractive plastic tablecloth.

I opened the book. I read: "Rainclouds over dark towers, rain falling in deep streets, a dark storm-beaten city of stone, through which one vein of gold winds slowly." The trials of an adolescent body went away, the literal drizzle falling on the real streets of Newcastle-under-Lyme receded, the passing streets of red-brick terraces and slate-clad maisonettes were abolished. This was the voice I hadn't heard since Narnia; the lovely, sure storytelling voice that, because of some temporarily perfect fit between teller and hearer, can talk a world into existence, and have you crave a fictive life that seems clearer in its lines and stronger in its colors than your own unnarrated existence. Immediately, I could see it, the line of bright gold creeping in a view like a smeared dim crystal, and as the book drew me in through this porthole to elsewhere, and carried me closer, so that I could make out that the gold beneath the rain's tarnish was a procession, of yellow-clad jugglers and merchants and musicians, led by a king "with leggings of saffron leather and a peaked yellow cap," I discovered that as well as being visually vivid in a way that made the rest of SF look like a stack of charcoal briquettes, this story, compared to most SF, returned me to emotional reality too, where actions had consequences that mattered, and situations were not as flimsy as thoughts, to be crumpled up and replaced by another if they displeased you. But the emotions in question were of a kind that needed SF's freedom to invent, in order for them to exist: SF's power to stipulate a whole worldful of probabilities, this time governing, not just the flashy stuff, but the subtle logic gates controlling emotional cause and effect.

The Left Hand of Darkness was about gender, and about perceiving the unity of humanity beneath the male–female difference. On the wintry planet of Gethen, however, where the procession wound through dark streets, this unity was made into a physiological fact. The narrator, an offworld diplomat named Genly Ai, was the only man on the planet; the Gethenians, red-brown, with faces as impassive as a cat's or an otter's, were human but androgynous. For twenty-two days of the month they were neuter. Then, for one week of estrus, they could be either male or female, and every individual had been both, unpredictably, many times over in the course of their adult life. They see the permanently male Mr. Ai, sent to make first contact

with them, as an ugly and perverted being, locked into one
small phase of sexuality like a person with, say, a foot fetish.
In turn Ai—perhaps more than is quite credible in someone
selected for this particular mission—finds it almost impossible
to hold their doubleness in his mind. For him, they flicker backward and forward between being men and being women; and in
the single case where he has a relationship on the planet that
approaches intimacy, with the king's Prime Minister, Estraven,
he is repelled. "As I sipped my smoking sour beer I thought that
at table Estraven's performance had been womanly, all charm
and tact and lack of substance, specious and adroit. Was it in
fact this soft supple femininity that I disliked and distrusted in
him? For it was impossible to think of him as a woman, that
dark, ironic, powerful presence near me in the firelit darkness,
and yet whenever I thought of him as a man I felt a sense of
falseness, of imposture . . ."

Of course, the novel is constructed so that, after many polit-
ical misadventures, including a labor camp for Ai and exile for
Estraven, the two should end up making a desperate escape
together across the planet's northern ice cap, in a tiny tent in
which there is no room for evasion or misunderstanding to continue. The moment of reconciliation that completes the arc of
the story comes when Ai looks across the stove and finds that
Estraven's face

in the reddish light was as soft, as vulnerable, as remote
as the face of a woman who looks at you out of her
thoughts and does not speak. And then I saw again, and
for good, what I had always been afraid to see, and had
pretended not to see: that he was a woman as well as
a man. Any need to explain the sources of that fear

vanished with the fear; what I was left with was, at last, acceptance of him as he was . . .

Now he sees the wholeness of his friend, a whole set of apparent dualisms that have puzzled him in the mythology and religion of Gethen resolve themselves. White and black, snow and the human shadow on the snow, prove to be halves of a single yin and yang–like unity. The gulf between Ai and Estraven is only the elemental difference between Self and Other. The left hand of darkness is light.

This was a piece of symbolism I found very powerful, and Le Guin had inlaid it in the details of Gethen's invented culture with a beautiful intricacy, so that they made a gloriously congruent sense in retrospect. Now it was clear why the Gethenian word for "pride" also meant "shadow"; why it was taboo on Gethen to offer advice. But the clarity of the recognition Le Guin had arranged between Ai and Estraven was designed to be so symbolically resonant that it went well beyond what you could imagine happening to people, of any gender, off the page. It went beyond conventional characterization. Solving the friendship solved the world. Le Guin used the fullness and power of her storytelling voice to get here. It was eloquent, elegant, slightly old-fashioned. Where most SF prose aimed to be instant and colloquial, hers was ceremonious; it deliberately borrowed authority from the kind of storytelling that this-worldly diplomats and explorers and anthropologists used to do, in the days when it was assumed that interpreting strangeness was a literary task as well as an academic or a purely practical one. Ambassadors to the court of the Tsar have waited for audience in icy antechambers, as Genly Ai does. Explorers in the Arctic and Antarctic have crept across ice caps under the iron laws of necessity, as Ai and Estraven do. Le Guin used the authority of her voice to make sure that the events she described were vividly present for the reader, thoughts and actions and sensations unspooling confidently into existence, denoted as crisply as footprints in snow; but when she wanted to fix the meaning of a situation, she pushed description, and pushed it and pushed it, not exactly into the abstract, but until it attained a state of rich pattern. This suited me. It was a way of arriving at emotional depth and complexity that did not depend on being able to apprehend them from less stylized, therefore more fragmentary realities.

Later, Le Guin began to worry that by using the grave certainties of these old kinds of storytelling, she had bought into a hierarchic, male-centered view of the world indissolubly associated with them. *The Left Hand of Darkness* was published in 1969. Genly Ai's phobic idea of femininity, "all charm and . . . lack of substance," and his fear of being attracted to the woman in Estraven in case he found himself fancying the man in him too, were pretty much commonplaces when she first gave them to him, but they dated fast. Feminist critics of Le Guin's work in the seventies pointed out some more systematic skews in it. She always, they said, picked a lonely, noble male character—a diplomat, a scientist—whenever she wanted to represent the *I* who got to deal with alien Otherness, as if normal, ordinary humanity had to be male. And because she had decided to refer to everyone on her planet of androgynes as "he," when you read *The Left Hand of Darkness* you effectively thought of Gethen as a world populated exclusively by men, with a few extra characteristics that are presented as their disturbing, alien aspect; in the yin-yang unity of the sexes on Gethen, the female half of Gethenians always figures as the darkness (intuitive, indirect, hidden, mysterious) and their male half as the light (rational, open, active, public). She'd set out to write a fable of gender unity, but she'd written it within a framework that took male primacy for granted.

Le Guin accepted these criticisms. For a time, starting in the late 1970s, she treated the power of her storytelling voice to say this is so, that is so, as an implicit surrender to a patriarchal agenda, and tried to purge it by writing deliberately decentered books, without the shapes of strong story in them. The result was probably the weakest period of her career since her early apprenticeship. Lately, thank heavens, she has decided that the power she tried to do without is more of a neutral tool than she had feared, and also a less dispensable part of her gifts as a writer. In her most recent books, the old voice is back, doing new things, the worry at its power conquered. But I never worried when I read *The Left Hand of Darkness*. I was male, and I took a romantic vision with male selfhood at its center straight to heart, as a beautiful fit with my own romantic wishes. I had been at single-sex schools for five years. Girls were just as alien to me by now as a hermaphroditic Prime Minister on skis. My encounters with them were clumsy and blurted. I would have liked it if they could have been complete and mythically resonant, like Genly Ai's reconciliation with Estraven, and I was grateful to Ursula Le Guin for creating me a model of the gender divide with such lucid, ideal architecture. By the time I finished *The Left Hand* I had a new favorite writer.

And after I had read *The Dispossessed,* the other great book from her predoubting period, I positively venerated her. *The Left Hand of Darkness* might offer a world whose symbolism was ideally clear, but this book brought me something altogether more sweeping: the lure of utopia. It was set on a dusty, desert moon two centuries into an experiment in communist anarchy. The hero, Shevek, was a great physicist who had some trouble, growing up, with the social conformity his society used instead of laws. People weren't supposed to resent the individuality of his mind, but they did. I responded to this: the clever person misunderstood was a theme I always had time for. But *The Dispossessed* seemed to offer a cure as well. On Anarres, no one owned anything, or wanted to. They worked for love at the jobs they could do best, or at the tasks their consciences told them were most urgent. When they needed a new jacket or an eiderdown they went to the public depot and picked one up. There was no money, and no government, just a committee anyone could sit on that coordinated the society's conversation with itself. But against all these negatives—and an environment whose sparseness and harshness was lovingly evoked—there was one great shining positive—solidarity. The people of Anarres had empty hands but open hearts. On Anarres, everyone belonged, even Shevek, who visited the world his ancestors had exiled themselves from and discovered that Anarres's bareness was fuller, for him, than any amount of comfort or plenty that depended on the division of people, one from another, by greater and lesser amounts of authority, or greater and lesser amounts of property. People did not always like each other, where Shevek came from, but they *recognized* each other, and gave without measure in order to receive without stint. They displayed an aristocratic disdain for the idea of grubbing around to balance the gifts they had given against the ones they had received. "We have no states, no nations, no presidents, no premiers, no chiefs, no generals, no bosses, no bankers, no landlords, no wages, no charity, no police, no soldiers, no wars. Nor do we have much else. We are sharers, not owners . . ."

Recitations like this could move me nearly to tears, when I was sixteen, and even transcribing these words now my eyes prickle at the memory of feeling that there was an ideal life next door, terribly close, kept from us all only by a few things we needed to discard; that the world could be radiant, if only we let it.

It is not an accident that Shevek's roll call of things that did not exist on his planet sounds so much like Henry James's list of the things absent on the American scene, and glows with the same confidence in the secret, or the joke, that makes apparent emptiness brim over with possibility. It's not an accident, any more than it is accidental that the towns of Anarres, on the map that I pored over, named Wide Plains and Elbow and Northsetting and Round Valley, lay alone on dusty prairies. They came from the same impulse that founded real American towns, the same specifically American perception about what may be built in a new place where the past's rules can all be abandoned. Only here, *ought* reigned completely, transmogrifying the white houses of De Smet into dormitories, the restaurants into public dining rooms, the motel into a communal bathhouse, and abolishing the shops altogether, as grotesque offenses to the human spirit. *The Dispossessed* returned me to the question that the stories of the town had posed, as I started to look around in the wider world, and gave a new, absolute answer, one that abolished the question. How shall I be fed by strangers? Simple: there are no strangers. Everyone is a brother or sister, everyone is as unconditionally committed to each other as family. Oh, how I wanted this! There are other themes in the novel, which meant much less to me at the time: it is also, for example, a book written in praise of committing yourself to passing time, and proudly allowing the strains of loyalty to a partner or a child to weather you, so that you wear time unashamedly on your face.

At sixteen I could hardly imagine the first phase of adulthood, let alone the later ones, and I had no idea how provocative it was in American terms—in its own way, an equally utopian proposition—to describe Shevek's partner, in her thirties, cheerfully losing teeth and collecting wrinkles. I ached to sit on golden grass on a day of celebration, eating little cakes prepared by the syndicate of cooks. I wanted to wander through a city without a single locked door. I wanted, as I had not wanted since I wanted Narnia, to *be* there; not because there was beautiful, this time—in fact it was aggressively unbeautiful—but because there my solitude could end. There, the walls that guarded it would all fall down. I longed for Anarres.

And this was strange, on the face of it, because I already lived in a dormitory, and I hated it. I hated having no privacy. I avoided washing on weekdays so that I wouldn't have to strip in the grim, carbolic-smelling basement bathroom of my boarding-house at school, where three metal bathtubs stood in a row without any partitions between them. Brotherhood, schmother-hood: other people scattered used football socks and wanked at night when you had to listen to them. I spent most of my time clenching my pores closed so that the collective life couldn't get in. Undisturbed solitude, with a lockable door, was the greatest luxury I could imagine. The difference about Anarres was that there I could imagine a world beyond my solitude that I could open up to in the confidence that it would match how I felt inside. It would be a warmed world, and my wishes would flow out to join millions of other wishes, all aimed at obtaining the specific set of joyous sensations that *The Dispossessed* described, in the unanimity that only fiction makes possible.

I decided that I was an anarchist. Maybe absolute politics of all kinds call most seductively to you when you're this age.

Of all things, it would be hardest then to be a pragmatist, comfortably aware that the street is full of people pretty much, though not exactly, like you, whose lives are just as important to them as yours is to you. Remember how unbearable the adults you knew best had become, just then? How repetitive and mechanical and maddening they seemed, stuck in a loop of behavioral tics and unvarying sayings, like Talking Action Man after the string in his back was pulled? When the subjectivities of other people jostle you so oppressively, it's hard to accept that what you see is, essentially, what you're going to get. You welcome systems and causes that can hold off this knowledge, especially those that give ideas priority over observation. If ideas take precedence, you can reconceptualize that mass of strangers as a humanity that demands that you take bold, radical action on its behalf. Several causes worked. I could have declared that I was an orthodox Communist, and let Marxist-Leninism abstract the crowd of other people for me into dialectically struggling classes, or maybe I could have taken Ayn Rand to heart, and seen the world through her eyes, split between heroic titans and conformist ants. I couldn't have been a fascist or a White Power advocate: those systems ooze unmistakable hate, and you have to be able to tell yourself, at sixteen, that your utopian urge is generous.

I certainly didn't find much to confirm my particular choice of utopia when I went out looking for corollaries to Anarres among real anarchists, in London, in 1980. British anarchism was going through a quiet patch. Punk's burst of enthusiasm for anarchist ideas and images was fading away; the age of road protests and illegal raves had not begun. Crusties had not yet been invented. So there was no real air of confrontation about anarchism just then; the movement was in the hands of elderly, transparently nice people who were activists for community gardening, and had once had a refugee from the Spanish Civil War to stay in their spare bedroom in Hemel Hempstead. Every two weeks, the anarchist newspaper *Freedom* would come out, with a front-page story that started from an item of current news, and always proved within three paragraphs that the solution to whatever-it-was lay in the complete abolition of government and private property. *Freedom* was published from the Freedom Bookshop, a venerable place up an alley in White-chapel, where Peter Kropotkin himself, in exile from the Tsar, had walked and talked. Kropotkin's pamphlets were still on sale in their original 1890s editions, now priced at 10p (25¢). His face twinkled down from a poster, saying, "Don't forget mutual aid, comrades!" I would bunk off sports, and go to Whitechapel in my school uniform. "D'you think there'll be a revolution soon?" I asked the volunteer behind the till. "I certainly hope so," he said. "I'm eighty-one."

But anarchism had a couple of points in its favor that were very important to me. In the first place, it uttered a great big, non-negotiable, rejectionist Fuck You to authority, as manifested in my life by school rules and housemasters. Punk gave me the soundtrack; my copy of the Fontana *Anarchist Reader,* edited by George Woodcock, equipped me with a whole set of grandly refusing words from history. "Whoever puts his hand on me to make me obey, is a tyrant," wrote Enrico Malatesta. "No God or master!" went the anarchist battle cry in the Spanish Civil War, even more concisely. This almost autistic view that any law would be oppression, any touch would be a violation, certainly matched my sense of myself at fifteen and sixteen, which was brittle, and melodramatic because brittle. I could believe that being told what to do might scatter me into atoms. It seemed quite possible that a dreadful dissolution would follow if I once let myself get claimed by any hand that had the power to join me into anything larger than myself. I might be carried over a brink into darkness, a darkness like the darkness inside Wally's mouth. I did not think about what other things, besides authority, depend on you allowing the touch of another person's hand to have power. I welcomed anarchism's perpetual shout of Hands Off.

Secondly, anarchism was secretly reassuring. It let you claim a wicked reputation as an enemy of humanity, an acolyte of destruction, while all the while being virtuous within its rind of apparent menace. It was like the anarchist flag. The true banner of anarchy, carried through the streets of Moscow in 1921 at the funeral of Kropotkin, is plain black. It is a deliberately blank square in the traditional color of evil, as lightless as a sample of the air in a cellar. It symbolizes pure negation. It doesn't care that it looks devilish; it knowingly sops up all the fear it may inspire as a conscious rejection of morality. But its devotees fly it in the confidence that it negates only the illusory and oppressive definitions of virtue put about by church and capital; that it is in fact a loud assertion of human goodness. The whole theory of anarchism actually depends upon a very innocent belief in the natural goodness of human beings. It wants to throw all laws away because it assumes that people do not have any innate drives toward dominance or cruelty. Those things, it says, are only effects of a cruel superstructure laid down over our kind biology. Far from being nasty and brutal and in need of restraint, people are fundamentally cooperative and altruistic, and if you just took away their chains, they would organize themselves spontaneously into a society as rich and intricate as the furled petals of a rose. I liked this. It suited my lingering anxiety about what might be concealed beneath my conscious thoughts to deny that anything was, at all: that I even had an unconscious, or any dark recess of my mind whose darkness could not be blamed on the effects of capitalism. Three cheers for the lovely black flag!

After a while the thrill began to wear off the sentences in Ursula Le Guin that had seemed most meaningful to me, and given me the most concentrated pleasure. I started to think that when she flew to the heights of patterning metaphor, perhaps the intensity she got was not completely earned. I went through one of her short stories in *Orsinian Tales,* a book set in an imaginary Eastern European country, attempting to snip off the most excessive phrases, in the hope that something to which I could give credence again would be left afterward. "Under their voices, the deep, weak singing voice of Kasimir's fiddle went on wordless," I read; I crossed out "like a cry from the depths of the forest." But the story just kept getting smaller.

Never mind; a lot of books can be read in a utopian way, if you put your mind to it. The coherence of story itself can offer a geography in which you can imagine yourself belonging more than you do in the mundane, disappointing world. In story, you can imagine being understood as a character is understood by a reader. There was an urban legend going around about that time, about a fanatical fan of *Watership Down* who jumped to his death off a multistory car park, in the hope that he'd be reincarnated as a rabbit. If such a person had actually existed, what he would have wanted would presumably have been access to the ordered story-world invented by Richard Adams, rather than life on all fours with a twitching, sensitive nose. In the same way, Trekkies who crave an existence in the Star Fleet future are proposing a life whose grammar is as firm and decisive as an interchange between Commander Ryker and Counselor Troi as they walk down a corridor of the *Enterprise,* a camera on a dolly retreating in step with them, and the corridor roofless, so that studio lamps subtly aligned can paint the actors' uniforms in ideal, even colors. The idea of living like a story is utopian in itself, when you're waiting for life to begin.

The waiting, the waiting. "Maybe tomorrow / Maybe some day ..." sang Chrissie Hynde on the radio, in "Talk of the Town." I loved that single; I coveted its world-weariness, because to sound so rueful about love, you had to have had it, and lost it, and maybe found it again, and every phase of the history the song looked back on, happy or sad, implied living fully in the world, being fully committed. My life seemed like limbo in comparison. The trembling sense I'd felt at thirteen, that huge feelings were imminent, was now a constant companion, a yearning buzz you wouldn't have known I felt if you'd seen me awkwardly hunched in my oversize overcoat. Sometimes I got impatient with it. I wanted something more immediate than a perpetual, wavering awareness of possibility. This was where cult books came in usefully. *The Doors of Perception, The Glass Bead Game, Zen and the Art of Motorcycle Maintenance,* Tom Robbins's *Another Roadside Attraction,* Philip K. Dick, some books by Kurt Vonnegut and Thomas Pynchon, the entire works of Jack Kerouac: they let you abort waiting, and take immediate delivery of some potent, if perhaps trashy, image of a counterlife, a freer and stranger existence, whether it was an imaginary, austere far-future monastery (Herman Hesse), or in the Beats' 1950s America, where driving furiously to Pittsburgh in an old Buick accelerated your soul. "Don't you know that God is Pooh Bear?" it said on the last page of *On the Road*—a sentence that, even when I was reading it with great satisfaction, stoned, in a friend's father's post-divorce bachelor pad in Cadogan Square, with Captain Beefheart playing on the stereo, I knew meant absolutely nothing.

One thing I never did was to fix my wishes on a single book. I never performed the kind of obsessive reading that lone gunmen seem so fond of, with their uncanny, consensual choice of Salinger's *Catcher in the Rye* for their One Book. Reading is no longer an exploratory act when it settles, in this way, on one text that no other can rival, or approximate, or even be allowed to resemble. It declares: this is the Truth, this is Me, astonishingly anticipated to the extent that this book has actually been waiting for me to come along and gaze into it and discern a complete, authoritative, quasi-scriptural reflection of myself. Both Mark Chapman, assassin of John Lennon, and John Hinckley, who tried to impress Jodie Foster by shooting Ronald Reagan, felt that J. D. Salinger's first-person narration by Holden Caulfield expressed their natures better than any of the thoughts in their own heads did. His stream of consciousness was more theirs than theirs was. So, because their own central sense of self was weak, they borrowed his, which, though fictional, seemed to have as definite an existence as the well-thumbed paperback in their windbreaker pocket, and made Holden an armature around which they could wind their obsessions.

The obvious irony here is that Holden Caulfield is an archetype of sympathetic wavering: the preppy on the loose in New York, ricocheting about in the bewildering space between childhood and adulthood, he decides that people are phony and then unmakes the decision, is repelled and then attracted without knowing why, a moment later, observed all the while by the adult consciousness of Salinger, which makes no explicit sound, but controls Holden's voice, and sees further than Holden does what emergent shape his adventures have. Every adolescent boy who reads the book feels a bit like him, but usually you feel that he's doing being a lost boy more completely than you, with a fictive conviction and wholeheartedness. You have to be *really* fucked-up to feel something stabilizing in your resemblance to him.

Another irony, more general, is present too. The ability to feel you have a special bond with the protagonist of a bestseller is dependent on the segregation of readers that is designed into books by their form. Books are a mass medium, but there is no way for readers to be aware of one another. The lines of attention run from reader to book, never laterally from reader to reader. A reader feels alone in a book, but is actually one of a crowd, all occupying the same points in textual space, all making a hubbub that none of them can hear. If the readers of *Catcher in the Rye* were visible to each other, it would become clear that the solitary paths of Holden's thoughts are actually intensively trafficked. Imagine the endless parking lots, the turnstiles, the take-a-number machines, the endless queues of pissed-off youth, with their long hair, short hair, greasy hair, confrontationally shaved hair, their combat jackets and anoraks and golf club blazers sarcastically worn; all of them, John Hinckley and Mark Chapman mere dots in the throng, all shuffling forward to take their turn at the front end of the attraction, where each reader steps up and looks through Holden Caulfield's eyes, at a room in a house in Pennsylvania on an icy evening in the 1940s, a room whose other occupant, a flu-gripped teacher, has no idea he is speaking to a million people. "'I'd like to put some sense into that head of yours, boy. I'm trying to help you. I'm trying to *help* you, if I can.' He really was, too. You could see that. But it was just that we were too much on opposite sides of the pole, that's all."

I wasn't single-minded enough to be a lone gunman. I wasn't looking for one perfect reflection of myself in a character. For me, the promise of books lay in them being multiple. They were inexhaustible because, turning disappointed or self-disgusted away from one book, you could always hope that the next would hit just the right spot, and remind you why you kept reading.

Instead, I discovered metafiction: stories about stories. The first monument of adult literature I discovered for myself was not Jane Austen at thirteen, but, at seventeen, the dull-green-spined Penguin Modern Classics edition of the collected stories of Jorge Luis Borges. Borges took me to a place where dry, crabbed, pedantic phrases could be the language of wonder. He made annotation into a technique of shimmering paradox. His footnotes had no bottom to them: you could fall through, and keep falling, tumbling without end into an abyss of recursive possibilities. *Reference* was the essence of what he did, pointing your attention from one apparently existing thing to another one, but it was always unreliable, because so many of the books, persons, places, flowers, gems, ideas he named were invented by him, glimmering into existence for just that moment at which he referred to them; and so many of the boxes he suggested you open were either empty, or contained an infinitely nested set of other ever-smaller boxes, or were larger on the inside than the outside, or, strangest of all, had no inside at all. In "The Garden of Forking Paths," he proposed a novel in which, at every point of decision, *both* outcomes took place, until the book contained "a growing, dizzying web of divergent, convergent and parallel times." In "The Library of Babel," he sketched—or rather, "adumbrated," to use one of the words from his mannered, repetitive vocabulary of favorites—a universe consisting entirely of ventilation shafts and hexagonal galleries, lined with identical volumes, whose pages contain every conceivable permutation of the 26 letters of the alphabet as they can be arranged at random over 410 pages. But not in order; the books are shuffled at random, and a librarian can walk for many miles over many years to find a single intelligible sentence, knowing all the while that, because the library comprises all possible permutations, it must therefore include

the detailed history of the future, the autobiographies of the archangels, the faithful catalogue of the library, thousands and thousands of false catalogues, the proof of the falsity of those false catalogues, a proof of the falsity of the *true* catalogue, the gnostic gospel of Basilides, the commentary upon that gospel, the commentary on the commentary on that gospel, the true story of your death, the translation of every book in every language, the interpolations of every book into all books . . .

Borges's characteristic maneuver was a version, in story, of the Möbius twist that the mathematical philosophers had discovered early in the twentieth century. Hoping to put logic on a foundation of consistent, comprehensive axioms, Bertrand Russell found instead that the ability of a set to include itself as a member set off a rip in the axiomatic fabric into which the whole hope for reliable, consistent knowledge was then inexorably sucked, like a black hole devouring the philosophic space. Later, Kurt Gödel showed that even the simplest mathematical system, like arithmetic, had the potential to eat its own tail in the same way, and therefore could not be proved to map reality reliably. Borges haunted these points of conceptual unmaking, using the power of the authorial voice to be both within the story and (simultaneously) its external sustainer, as his analogue of Russell's problem, and thus the means to pry open a vortex. Into the classification system of an imaginary Chinese encyclopedia, he introduced the category of "things contained in this encyclopedia," a part which must therefore contain the whole, which in turn must contain the part, that contains the whole, ad infinitum; and this was just one of his most modest and local embodiments of the idea. Here, in Borges's work, story became almost pure form. It contained just enough substance—just enough naming and evocation—to furnish the ideas with a backing, like the film of mercury on the back of a mirror that allows a flat thing to contain ever-receding depths. Borges's stories actually reached the state that the dumbest idea-led science fiction only approximated to. They were truly about something other than people. They were about themselves, about the interesting diagrams that the multiplicity of things books do will make, if you reduce them to pure lines and angles: perfect reading, in a way, for Piaget's last age, of "abstract operations."

They seduced me; and when prolonged exposure to Borges's unchanging circuit of preoccupations had left me feeling bleak, I could turn to metafiction's European branch, represented by Italo Calvino, where the residual human content backing the lovely forms was a little bit warmer, a little bit more conversational and expansive. I collected the thin, elegant Picador translations of his books. The conceptual cities of *Invisible Cities* were limpidly beautiful. *If On a Winter's Night a Traveler* managed to proceed, conjuriously, by sampling for you the different types of pleasure that you, the book's reader, might obtain from the first chapters of ten different novels you stumbled across in the fruitless search to get hold of a copy of *If On a Winter's Night a Traveler.* It sounded, from time to time, as if

Calvino was regretting language's inadequacy to convey the world; but in fact, at these moments, he was always slyly demonstrating how, by slitting an incision in one level of representation, and pulling through the one below in a decorative rosette, he could replace dull old, mute old, heavy old material reality, and have language do everything that atoms used to. "To tell it as I would like," he wrote in *The Non-Existent Knight*, the story of an empty suit of armor in the service of Charlemagne,

> this blank page would have to bristle with reddish rocks, flake with pebbly sand, sprout sparse juniper trees. In the midst, on a twisting ill-marked track, I would set Agilulf, passing erect on his saddle, lance at rest. But this page would have to be not only a rocky slope but the dome of the sky above, so low that there is room only for a flight of cawing rooks in between. With my pen I should also trace faint dents in the paper to represent the slither of a snake through grass or a hare crossing a heath . . .

I had always reduced books to pattern in my memory, preferring the inside curves of story to the difficulties of engagement with the things the story represented. Now, I had found stories that were pure pattern already; that took the pleasures I had enjoyed in *The Silver Chair* and *The Voyage of the Dawn Treader*, and twisted them around on themselves, till they met their own beginnings in a sealed, self-conscious loop of narration that needed nothing outside itself.

Utopias took away everything discreditable about humanity. The black flag absorbed destructive impulses while it denied them. The textual abyss swallowed the whole world. To chart my mind's geography at eighteen, imagine that in the place where a clearing in the forest had once been, and then an island in the sea of possibilities, and then a busy town on the lonely prairie, the space that books made in me now centered on a sinkhole, a circular gap in the fabric, that sucked troubling emotion into itself. But at the same time that I found meta-fiction, I discovered another kind of writing, in which the holes weren't abstract at all, in which nothingness became hot and fleshy: porn, of course.

In the early 1980s, when I began reading one-handedly, the present incredible profusion of "erotic novels" didn't yet exist. The first dirty book I tried was the novel of *Emmanuelle.* It didn't do much for me. It still had some connection to reality, it still had a faint intention to represent something, a milieu of chic hedonism among the minor French diplomats and swinging air hostesses of Bangkok, circa 1970. The people in *Emmanuelle* were just real enough to waken my real-world sense of judg-ment. They obliged you to notice that they were boring air-heads. While you waited for them to have sex, you had to listen to them talk drivel. This was not what I wanted pornography to be. I had no wish for books that resembled, or mimicked, or sup-plemented my own gauche experience of sex. By then the wait-ing was over. I had made some actual love with an actual female person, and I had discovered that, whether you were feeling kind or feeling edgy, feeling bored or feeling excited, there was nothing like real sex for driving you out of your head and into your skin, for stopping you caring about conceptual geography, for delivering you both, sweating and trembling, to the heart of reality, to reality at its most consequential, where you feel your heart beating, and know that your finite number of heartbeats really ought to be laid out on the pursuit of happiness. Sex made you feel terminally alive. In short, real sex turned out to be the quintessence of the kind of connected experience I had always looked to books to counterbalance. If I was going to read about sex, I wanted it to be a kind of sex that exploited text's liquid ability to do things that reality didn't; more than that, I wanted it to exert, like the other kinds of reading that had hooked me, a pressure that kept reality at bay. And I wanted it to elicit and enact and soak up the emotions from the sump of my psyche that I would not dare to allow near a real person. C. S. Lewis once praised tales of the marvelous, which are "actual additions to life; they give, like certain rare dreams, sensations we never had before, and enlarge our conception of the range of possible experience." *That* was what I wanted porn to be. *Emmanuelle* failed the test comprehensively.

But then, in Heffers bookshop in Cambridge, I chanced on a series of Grove Press paperbacks that claimed to be suppressed Victorian classics. These American imports were packaged in chocolate-box colors and trimmed with curly Art Nouveau type, in line with the marketing ploy. Each had a woman's name as a title ("Beatrice," "Davina") and a gauzy photo of a 1970s nymph looking wistfully nude in a field of poppies. Very Athena poster, very shampoo ad. On the inside, however, there was nothing soft-focus about the way they conjured up female bodies in prose. The writing grabbed at what it described. It grasped it, it squeezed it. It evoked flesh as if to pinch it between noun and adjective. It took exact, almost obsessional note of different kinds of tissue: the berrylike crimping of a nipple, the rubbery knot of a navel, the smooth weight of a thigh. It looked at the colors of bodies, and even at the colors of the shadows on them, specifying cinnamon highlights, ginger-shaded clefts, pubic hair in tight yellow curls.

I recognized this. It was another manifestation of the greed for particulars I had always sought out in stories. And now the greedy story had become angry too. It was not just that these books were as eager for punishments as for actual sex: the anger was intrinsic, it was written into the way the luscious female bodies were seen in the first place. To the eye of this kind of story, the curves of a woman were imbued with a scarcely tolerable power, which intensified the more voluptuous she was, the more closely she approximated to porn's anatomically unlikely ideals of bulbousness. Women inspired desire by being the objects, of all the objects in the world, in which the Keatsian delights of texture and color and scent were most concentrated; the warm and bountiful surfaces against which you most wanted to press and huddle. More than that: they broadcast desire, they *did* desire *to* men, and so to you, the male reader, when they were evoked on the page. But at the same time, they thwarted desire, by not quite being objects at all, by not being as open to possession as all the other objects that they exceeded in desirability. They weren't biteable like apples, they weren't driveable like cars. It was as if women were playing an unfair trick, and they did it, this invidious, provocative withholding of themselves, merely by being people. The solution was to push into them; to cram the omnipotent imaginary dick with which porn equipped its reader, into the three openings in them about which porn was interchangeably excited, making them all hole. Porn first worked itself (and me) into excited fury by conjuring women's bodily frontiers. Then it breached them. Farther up and farther in!—as it said in the Narnia books. This vengeful wish didn't have to be embodied in a literal rape fantasy. In fact, I avoided the books that were crass enough and guileless enough to make me notice that that's what it amounted to. Anger could perfectly well be worked out in fucks that looked rapturously consenting. The force was already there in the language, which at these moments of resolution deliberately crossed the line separating the words properly used to describe people from those used to denote things. The challenge for the pornographer was to go a fraction further than even their reader's most coldly assessing self expected, to produce a new shock of verbal reduction, and therefore a new sense of possession. Successful porn transfixed you at the same moment that, by one orifice or another, it invited you to transfix its imaginary harem.

So I read *Davina* and I read *Beatrice,* and without looking too closely at it I poured into them a jealous anger that went all the way back, I'm sure, to the (male) infant's first discovery that the warm breast they depend upon belongs to a person, who has the power to walk away. I read as if the fantasies the porn enacted were entirely the authors' responsibility, and vanished back between the covers when I shut the book, having rid me of something I didn't want to own. I would even, as a farewell to porn, play over what I'd just read from the point of view of the female character, letting my sense of outrage and resistance tell me that I was still a nice guy. Everything was hunky-dory. I knew that by reading these nasty and corrupted specimens of fiction I was deliberately betraying the things I honored in story. I knew that there was a blatant contradiction between this brutish thingifying of women, and my nervous attention to them as individuals in real life. But I didn't care. I wanted to be nasty. I wanted to transgress again, to go across this new line fiction offered me. Now, as well as loving books, and learning from them, I could consummate the relationship by having sex with them.

Only from time to time I began to find that the sharply gross phrases the porn came up with to seal my possession of its warm channel to nowhere left me feeling as if I had murdered someone. And soon I would discover that when a fantasy collapses, when the unreal estate you have been manipulating in the service of desire turns back to vacuum, and you find yourself confronting your own wishes undisguised by story, the encounter is not fun; for everything you put into a story, you store in yourself, there being no such thing in inner geography as a truly bottomless hole. Whatever you bury returns some day, to remind you of what you have left undone.

That's about it. Those are the origins of my life as a reader. Bridget died when she was twenty-two, of cystine deposits in her brain, an organ that can't be transplanted. "I'm sick of living at the frontiers of medical knowledge," she said soon before the end. She lingered long enough for my father to read her the whole of *The Lord of the Rings,* aloud. I went off to university, and there I met people whose privacy isn't mine to dispense with. So the rest is none of your business.

Except for this one scene, which repeats, in spite of all the self-knowledge I have ever been able to muster. I've fucked things up again. My heart is broken. I have lost my life's jewel. I am inconsolable. I go into a bookshop. And as I walk down the aisles, I remember that in every novel there are reverses, that all plots twist and turn, that sadness and happiness are just the materials authors use, in arrangements I know very well; and at that thought the books seem to kindle into a kind of dim life all around me, each one unfolding its particular nature into my awareness without urgency, without haste, as if a column of gray, insubstantial smoke were rising from it, softening the air, filling it with words and actions which are all provisional, which could all be changed for others, according to taste. Among these drifting pillars, the true story of my life looks no different; it is just a story among stories, and after I have been reading for a while, I can hardly tell anymore which is my own.

ACKNOWLEDGMENTS

■ ■ ■

Most of the books I used when writing this one are mentioned in the text, but I should also mention Jacqueline Rose's *The Case of Peter Pan; or, The Impossibility of Children's Fiction* (London, 1992); Sven Birkerts's *The Gutenberg Elegies* (New York, 1994); *The Cool Web: The Pattern of Children's Reading,* edited by Margaret Meek et al. (London, 1977); David Pears's wonderful *Wittgenstein* in the old Fontana Modern Masters series (London, 1971); Elizabeth Anscombe's *Collected Philosophical Papers,* vol. 2 (Oxford, 1981); and Arthur Applebee's *The Child's Concept of Story* (Chicago, 1978).

In random order but for unrandom acts of help and kindness and intellectual succor, I'd like to thank Edmund de Waal, Judith Maltby, Marina Benjamin, Jenny Uglow, Ian Hunt, David Sexton, Julian Loose and Kate Teltscher, Anne Malcolm, Simon Coates, "David in Cambridge," my parents, my grandmother, and Bridget Spufford (1967–1989). None of them are responsible for what I have chosen to say, and not say, here. In his other role as my editor at Faber, Julian Loose managed never to raise an eyebrow at the delays in the project, or its deviation from the outline we first discussed. In *his* other role as literary editor of the *Evening Standard,* David Sexton provided me with income, and stimulus, and indulgence through many procrastinations. Katie Campbell (God love her), deputy literary editor of the *Standard,* understood how freelancers feel about being paid. Jenny Turner commissioned an early version of Chapter One for the *Independent on Sunday.* Max Anderson reminded me of James Bond and suggested I look into the favorite reading of lone gunmen. Sarah Spankie sent me to Antarctica—a journey irrelevant to this book, but too large and permanent a joy not to thank her for it in print. Michael Watts of the *Mail on Sunday* sent me to De Smet, South Dakota, and the Laura Ingalls Wilder Memorial Society looked after me while I was there; Mr. Craig Munger was especially kind.

ABOUT THE AUTHOR

■ ■ ■

FRANCIS SPUFFORD, a London-based journalist and critic, is a contributor to *Granta* and *The Guardian*. For his first book, *I May Be Some Time,* he was named the London *Sunday Times* Young Writer of the Year and received the 1997 Somerset Maugham and Writers' Guild awards.